A Short History of Modern Leadership Theory

by

Dr. J. Robert Clinton
Associate Professor of Leadership
School of World Mission
Fuller Theological Seminary

ISBN 1-932814-18-3

Barnabas Publishers
2175 North Holliston Avenue
Altadena, CA 91001

A SHORT HISTORY OF MODERN LEADERSHIP THEORY

A Paradigmatic Overview of the Leadership Field

from 1841-1986

Abstract

This paper surveys the leadership field from 1841 to 1986 using time periods determined by dominant research paradigms. Five periods are identified: Phase I. Great Man Era-1841-1904, Phase II. Trait Era-1904-1948, Phase III. Behavior Era-1948-1967, Phase IV. Con- tingency Era-1967-1980, Phase V. Complexity Era-1980-1986. The survey identifies prominent leadership influentials, works, theories, and models for each of the periods. This paradigmatic analysis overviews the historical context so as to enable a student of leadership theory to study further leadership research and models in an integrated fashion. One result of this overview is a balanced categorization of leadership ele- ments. Ile major categories are then symbolized into a leadership equa- tion. This equation can be used as an integration and evaluation tool for leadership analysis.

Table of Contents

A SHORT HISTORY OF MODERN LEADERSHIP THEORY

A Paradigmatic Overview of the Leadership Field
From 1841–1986.

Direction of the Paper

Historically, from a paradigmatic viewpoint, modern leadership research and theory can be viewed in five phases:

>Phase I.   Great Man Era: 1841–1904
>Phase II. Trait Era: 1904–1948
>Phase III. Behavior Era: 1948–1967
>Phase IV. Contingency Era: 1967–1980
>Phase V.   Complexity Era: 1980–1986

Two items of that statement need further explaining—modern leadership research and theory, and paradigmatic viewpoint.

The scientific thinking process being introduced in the early nineteenth century began to impact people writing about leadership from the mid-1800s on. I call this the "Modern Leadership Research Era." It is characterized by at least two major influences. One, the scientific method of observation, deduction, and replication of findings prevailed as the more sophisticated approach to obtain truth. Two, modern communication networks began to build so that written information could be transmitted more readily. This meant that researchers could learn of other findings and build upon them. There was the possibility of connected threads of thinking in an area of study.

I am using paradigm to mean a dominant research approach which was followed by the majority of researchers during a given specified time period. I am using it somewhat analogously to Kuhn (1970). The identification of a dominant research approach and the tracing of it over a period of time until it no longer dominates underlies the fivefold outline given above. Usually a dominating research approach is replaced by another newer approach which seems better to answer the anomalies of a previous approach. When such a new paradigm comes in we describe this as a paradigm shift.[1] Sometimes remnants of the old remain. At other times the old is discarded. The study of leadership paradigms and paradigm shifts gives a broad contextual framework upon which a leadership student can build. Present day research is better understood in the light of this historic paradigmatic viewpoint.

This paper will develop this framework as an aid toward providing an overall context for examining leadership. In specific terms this paper intends to overview the history of leadership theory from the mid-1800s until 1986 with an aim toward

1. identifying the paradigmatic eras,

2. recognizing some prominent people from each era,

3. noting some important written works of each era,

4. pointing out some of the centers of influence of leadership theory,

5. describing the dominant models of each era,

6. defining important leadership terms from this paradigmatic overview.

Students preparing for the mission field, mid-career missionaries, and national leaders majoring in the School of World Mission leadership concentration are the intended audience for this paper. These students already have exercised leadership and will do so again, most in cross-cultural situations. In their new positions they will select and train emerging leaders. The responsibilities of such work demand people competent to lead. Such people need to be well grounded in the leadership field. We in the leadership concentration have determined that being well grounded means one should

1. be familiar with the overview of history of the field,

2. know the prominent people who have influenced the discipline,

---

[1] See Kuhn (1970) for development of paradigmatic theory. See Kraft (1977), Chapter 2. Mirrors of Reality, for application of the paradigm shift concept to ethnotheological concerns.

3. be at least familiar with and perhaps, further, know the prominent ideas, models and theories of the field,

4. know the kinds of leadership research that has been done and the trends toward future research,

5. be able to use perspectives from this overview to analyze leadership situations in other cultural situations.

This paper serves as a springboard to these ends.

I. INTRODUCTION

Anyone teaching in the leadership field should be familiar with an overview of what has happened historically in the field. This is not easy since leadership is a complex subject which has been studied for a long time, but only in the past one hundred and forty years (give or take a decade or two) has been evolving toward a scientific multi-discipline.[2] Part of its complexity lies in its interdisciplinary nature. There is no one specific discipline called leadership. It is a subject that stretches over many disciplines. The field has not been integrated under one rubric.

However, its development in the last one hundred fifty years is not unlike other disciplines which too were fragmented and fought to survive

---

[2] That the leadership field is a multi-discipline field was brought home to me in some recent research attempting to analyze backgrounds of prominent leadership people and departments through which these influential people communicated leadership information. I was amazed to discover that people influencing leadership come from such disciplines as: education, educational psychology, psychology, administrative science, industrial management, social psychology, behavioral psychology, industrial psychology, organizational sociology, sociology, management, etc. Departments through which leadership information was being communicated include: Administrative Sciences, Behavioral Sciences, Business Administration, Education and Organizational Behavior, Human Resources, Industrial Administration, Industrial Relations and Management, Industrial/Organizational Psychology, Management, Management and Organization Sciences, Management and Organizational Behavior, Management Science(s), Organization and Human Resources, Organizational Behavior, Organizational Behavior and Management, Organizational Sociology, Organization and Management, Personnel and Organizational Behavior, Psychology, Psychology and Industrial Relations, Psychology and Organizational Behavior, etc. I believe there is a need for diversity of perspectives as I shall say later in this paper. However, there is probably a greater need at the moment for a common core on leadership that one could expect all leadership students to know. Apparently such is not the case now.

as disciplines.[3] This introduction will suggest the nature and complexity of leadership. It will suggest a time-line approach for tracing leadership theory. Though oversimplified, it will prove helpful as a grid through which to see leadership evolving as a specific multi-disciplinary field.

A. The Nature and Complexity of Leadership

Stogdill begins his exhaustive treatment of leadership with these words which indicate that the fascination with leadership is not just a modern fad.

> The study of leadership is an ancient art. Discussions of the subject will be found in Plato, Caesar, and Plutarch, just to mention a few from the classical era. The Chinese classics are filled with hortatory advice to the country's leaders. The ancient Egyptians attributed three qualities of divinity to their king .... A scholarly highlight of the Renaissance was Machiavelli's **The Prince**, still widely quoted as a guide to effective leadership of sorts; it formed the basis for a modern line of investigation by Christie and Geis (1970) in their Mach scale. (Bass 1981:5)

Concerning the concept of leadership, he further states,

> Leadership appears to be a rather sophisticated concept. Words meaning head of state, military commander, princes, procon-sul, chief, or king are the only ones found in many languages to differentiate the ruler from other members of society. A pre-occupation with leadership as opposed to headship based on inheritance, usurpation, or appointment occurs predominantly in countries with an Anglo-Saxon heritage. The **Oxford English Dictionary** (1933) notes the appearance of the word "leader" in the English language as early as the year 1300. However, the word "leadership" did not appear until the first half of the nineteenth century in writings about political influence and control of British Parliament. (Bass 1981:7)

---

[3] See Langness (1974) whose study of culture theory traces the development of anthropological paradigms. Anthropology as a discipline struggled to develop as a discipline and to integrate its various paradigms.

Stogdill notes that the earliest literature on leadership was concerned almost entirely with theoretical issues. Note Machiavelli and Plato in that regard. Theorists sought to identify types of leadership and to relate them to the things happening in society. Further, they sought to account for the emergence of leadership by examining the qualities of the leader and the elements of the situation he faced. He noted that earlier theorists can be differentiated from more recent ones in two basic ways. They did not fully take into account the interaction between individual and situational variables, and they tended to develop more comprehensive theories than do recent students of leadership. (Bass 1981:5, 6)

Two quotes, one from Browne, a mid-twentieth century theorist, and one from Stogdill, the dean of leadership authors, not only indicate the complex nature of leadership but also point out the lack of integration and conclusiveness. Brown indicates some of the progress of leadership toward becoming a scientific discipline. Writing in the introduction to his overview of leadership literature in 1958, he observes movement toward a leadership research methodology which was more scientific.

For approximately fifty years, and particularly during the past twenty-five years, psychologists and sociologists have been increasingly active in attempting to introduce the methods and knowledge of the human sciences into the study of leadership. The theoretical framework of these human disciplines still is in the developmental stages, but it is being utilized in the leadership area, and it well may be that leadership studies will contribute eventually to the general theory of human science. It is too soon, however, for any highly effective coagulation of these more recent scientific attempts to study leadership. No successful attempt has been made to produce an over-all book or other comprehensive coordination on leadership studies because the material is still too much in a state of flux and confusion—there is much fluidity, but not a great amount of viscidity. (Browne 1958:iii)

In his preface, some sixteen years after Brown's optimistic forward look, Stogdill gives some rather discouraging comments concerning the progress of the discipline of leadership.

Four decades of research on leadership have produced a bewildering mass of findings. Numerous surveys of special problems have been published, but they seldom include all the studies available on a topic. It is difficult to know what, if anything, has been convincingly demonstrated by replicated research. The endless accumulation of empirical data has not produced an integrated understanding of leadership. There is a need for stocktaking—for an inventory of results. Leadership practice should be based on valid experimental findings. Future research should be designed to explore new problems rather than repeat what has been done in the past. Indeed, the desire to know is in itself sufficient justification for undertaking a comprehensive analysis of the literature on leadership. (Bass 1981: xvii)

Some, such as McCall and Lombardo (McCall et al 1978), almost despair that anything can be done to integrate such a diverse amount of sometimes contradictory evidence and ideas. Their book, **Leadership— Where else can we go?**, is a rather negative critical evaluation of where leadership has been and a brainstorming effort to suggest new directions that may be more fruitful.

I have just completed a leadership bibliographic research project.[4] Its findings have formed the basis for this paper. I have felt the confusion of this lack of integration as I have searched a massive amount of materials in the field of leadership. Yet I do see progress. What helped me see progress was the use of a time-line. I have found it helpful to use a time-line to organize what I was seeing. I broke the time-line up into development phases. Viewing the whole time-line and the significant boundary conditions, I was able to begin to integrate my understanding of the development of leadership theory. Let me first give a brief overview of the time-line. Then I shall make a second pass to give a more detailed breakdown of my identification of the boundary phases bordering the paradigm shifts.

B. Time-Line Analysis of Leadership Field

How does one get some perspective on a divergent non-integrated field such as leadership? I believe a first step is a historical time-line.

---

[4] "Reflections On A Leadership Bibliographic Search," 1986, unpublished doctoral paper in the School of World Mission of Fuller Theological Seminary.

Actually someone should do for leadership what Langness[5] has done for anthropology. The method we (at the SWM) used to study theory of anthropology (somewhat of an ethnohistorical approach)[6] needs to be done for leadership as a whole. Now Bass (1981)[7] has much of the data for this in his book, but the emphasis of a time-line approach is missing and one gets lost very quickly in the details. A historical time-line seeks to display the major periods or eras of significance. It is broken up into development phases. The development phases are defined by boundary conditions which signify transition times or movement from one research emphasis to another—that is, a paradigm shift.

Let me give the sequence of analysis that led me to Figure 5 which gives a simplified time-line containing five phases. The first major break is somewhere in the mid-1800s as seen in Figure 1.

---

5 This paper is a shortened form of the very thing I am suggesting. What is needed is a book length effort with detailed research into areas that I have simply surveyed. The results of this present paper have depended on the selectivity of materials available to me. Of approximately 1000 important bibliographic entries, I have located more than 70% in the Southern California libraries within an hour-and-a-half distance of Fuller. Detailed research would expand both the 1000 entries and the percentage of entries reviewed.

6 This course, MB730 Theory of Anthropology, deals primarily with the history of the field of anthropology. Dr. Alan Tippett, one of the early pioneers of modern missiology, has done fundamental work in ethnohistory which does longitudinal analysis as well as point analysis of history.

7 Stogdill wrote his **Handbook of Leadership** in 1974. After his death, Bass updated this work in 1981. His text is massive, 856 pages and a bibliography of more than 5000 entries. It is so comprehensive and refers to so many leadership issues, people, works, ideas, theories and models that it is difficult to get an overall grasp of leadership. The forest-for-the-trees syndrome prevails. Yet no person involved in leadership training can afford to be without it and to have interacted with its massive findings. Bass's "information power" is significant. What he selects (that is, includes or excludes) and how he interprets has far-reaching effects on the leadership field. His book will most likely be the only single text that all leadership students training in diverse fields will be exposed to.

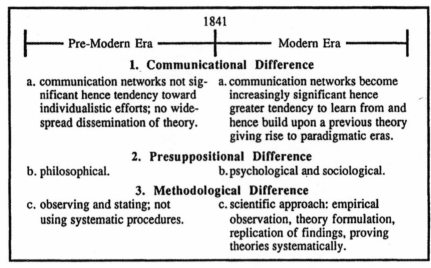

Figure 1. Paradigm Shift from Pre-Modern Era to Modern Era

The second major break occurred in 1948. The Trait Theory which had dominated the research approach for some forty years was proving to be a fruitless endeavor. A series of reviews of what had been accomplished during the Trait Era occurred in the mid-forties. Stogdill's paper concluded this trend of critically viewing the Trait Era. It brought about the major paradigm shift in the study of leadership. I will discuss his paper later when I give a detailed analysis of my identification of boundary conditions between paradigms. It is enough for now to simply recognize that leadership theory took a major turn, its most major shift, at that point.

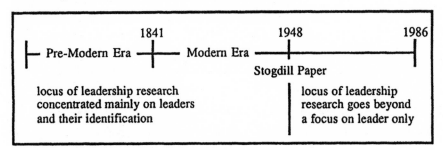

Figure 2. Major Paradigm Shift in Locus of Leadership Research

Stogdill's paper was originally entitled "Personal Factors Associated With Leadership: A Survey of the Literature" and was printed in the **Journal of Psychology,** 1948, 25, 35–71. When Bass (1981) revised Stogdill's magnum opus (1974) he included Stogdill's paper intact in Chapter 4 which he entitled "Leadership Traits: 1904–1947." Our timeline becomes altered in terms of paradigms as seen in Figure 3.

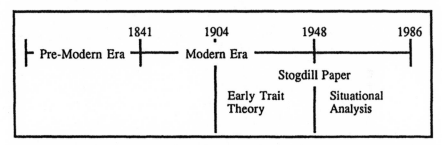

Figure 3. Trait Theory Era Identified

I will suggest two reasons for identification of the turn of the century as the beginning of the Trait Era when I give my detailed analysis of boundary conditions.

Prior to the turn of the century, theorists such as Carlyle, Galton, Woods and James concentrated on the study of "Great Men;" that is, people who had significantly affected history. I will discuss this era in more detail later. For now it is enough that we note the difference in this paradigm and the trait paradigm which followed it. Figure 4 illustrates this along the time-line.

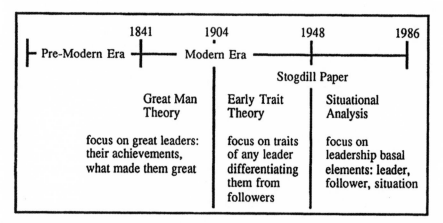

Figure 4. Major Research Foci: Great Man, Early Trait Era, Post-Stogdill

In line with Toffler's (1970) general observations[8] and Whitehead's acute paradigmatic insight[9] (Knowles 1980:), the pace of change

---

[8] Toffler's **Future Shock** stresses the importance of recognizing the pace of change.

[9] Alfred North Whitehead's observation, given at a commencement address at Harvard University in 1930, is worthy of note in this regard.

Throughout history, until the first quarter of the twentieth century, the life-span of an individual was less than the time-span of major cultural change. Under this condition it was appropriate to define education as a process of transmittal of what is known—of transmitting the culture. It was also appropriate to define the role of the teacher as that of transmitter of information and to regard education as an agency for youth . . . We are living in the first period of human history for which this assumption is false . . . Today this time span is considerably shorter than that of human life, and accordingly our training must prepare individuals to face a novelty of conditions.

Knowles adds further,

In other words, as the time-span of major cultural change has become shorter than the life-span of the individual, it becomes necessary to redefine education as a process of continuing inquiry. The role of the teacher must shift from that of transmitter of information to facilitator and resource to self-directed inquiry, and to regard increased much more rapidly. Great Man theory lasted about sixty-plus years. Early Trait[10] theory prevailed for about forty years. The next paradigm, the Ohio State research emphasis and its spin-offs, lasted for about twenty years. Fleishman's paper (1973)[11] described the thinking that led to that paradigm. Fiedler's contingency model (1967) and spin-offs or alternate situational models have dominated for almost fifteen years. And presently we are in an era of complex models. I will explain this hurried overview in more detail in the section which follows on boundary conditions. At this point in the paper, I am seeking to give a simplified overview of leadership history viewed paradigmatically. Figure 5 shows the complete time-line in simplified form. Later after detailed study of boundaries and phases, I will construct a fuller chart which includes not only the findings of Figure 5 but also several other important comparative categories.

---

education as a lifelong process. For knowledge gained at any point of time will become increasingly obsolete in the course of time. (Knowles 1980:40, 41)

The implications of this observation are slowly penetrating educational circles. The implications for training in this rapid pace of change as seen by Whitehead has had very little, if any, impact on theological education. This notion needs to be acknowledged and should dominate curriculum design in theological education.

10 Trait Theory is broken up into two categories. Early Trait Theory had as its focus the differentiation of traits between leaders and followers. It was the dominating research paradigm from 1904 to 1948. Latter Trait Theory had as its focus the identification of traits of leaders demonstrating successful behavior in various industrial leadership roles. It has not been a dominant paradigm but has persisted from the fifties to the present.

11 Fleishman's (1973) paper, "Twenty Years of Consideration and Structure," reveals the feelings of one who as an aspiring doctoral student experienced this paradigm shift. He writes in such a way as to describe the actual shifts, the prevailing view, the research that sparked the new paradigm and the outworking of the new paradigm.

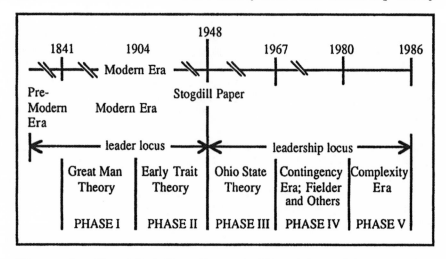

Figure 5. Simplified Paradigmatic Time-Line of Leadership Theory

II. DETAILED DISCUSSION OF PARADIGMATIC ERAS AND BOUNDARY CONDITIONS

In Section II, I will fill in more of the details of my analysis of the time-line. The generic term for a specific era is a development phase. The transition time between phases is called the boundary conditions. I shall here give a more detailed account of the boundary conditions. In Section III of this paper, I will pass through the development phases noting the significant people, works, and issues of the phases.

A. Phase I. The Great Man Era—1841–1904

It is easier to identify the development phases by seeing the boundary conditions between the phases. Once boundaries are identified, one can begin comparative studies between eras and can see unique characteristics of the different development phases.

Prior to 1840 (a very rough date) literature on leadership was concerned almost entirely with theoretical issues. Note Machiavelli and Plato in that regard.[12] Theorists sought to identify types of leadership and to relate them to the things happening in society. Students of leadership were generalists who theorized on leadership—what it ought to be. In the mid-1800s, increasingly the tendency became to observe not leadership per se but leaders. Leadership study was focused on leaders. Students sought to account for the emergence of leadership by examining the origins of the leader and the elements of the situation he faced.

Typical of this era of leadership study would be the following quote from Carlyle's **On Heroes and Hero-Worship** which typifies the era, and from which I derive the name of Development Phase I, The Great Man Era.

> For, as I take it, universal History, the history of what man has accomplished in this world, is at bottom the History of the Great Men who have worked here. They were the leaders of men, these great ones; the modellers, patterns, and in a wide sense creators, of whatsoever the general mass of men contrived to do or to attain; all things that we see standing accomplished in the world are properly the outer material result, the practical realization and embodiment, of Thoughts that dwelt in the great men sent into the world: the soul of the whole world's history, it may justly be considered, were the history of these." (Carlyle 1963:9)

This book was first published in 1841. In it Carlyle chooses six classes[13] of great men heroes, from widely-distant countries and epochs. Out of the Great Man era of leadership study came the familiar question, "Are leaders born or made?" Carlyle and others would say they are born and that they create the situation and progress for which they are noted. Others felt that it was the situation which set the stage for the Great Man to come to the fore. In either case, whether the leader was born or made,

---

[12] Plato (Bass 1981:17) generalized on the need for three kinds of leadership: (1) the philosopher-statesman to rule the republic with reason and justice; (2) the military commander to defend the state and enforce its will; (3) the businessman to provide for citizens' material needs and satisfy their lower appetites. The needs met his idealized version of what the perfect republic should be. Machiavelli debated philosophical power issues. His identification of two major power motivations, love and fear, still are referred to as basic in power theory today.

[13] See also Bass (1981) Chapter 2, "Types and Functions of Leadership."

the major methodology of study was biographical (or philosophical using biographical data).[14]

B. Boundary Between Great Man Era and Trait Era

The termination of this era of study is not so easy to see.[15] The study of leadership shaded over from just the study of Great Men into a search for the qualities commonly evinced in the lives of Great Men. I was helped in identifying the boundary by two items. One was Bass's title of Chapter 4 in his revised edition of Stogdill's handbook, Chapter 4, Leadership Traits: 1904–1947. Most likely Bass, who titled that chapter, based his dates on the availability of research papers. Probably the earliest available trait research paper dates back to 1904. I have not been able to verify this but think it a likely explanation. I will return to this item when I identify the end of the Trait Era. A second item that helped me identify the beginning of the Trait Era, and more specifically why there was a shift, is an excerpt from Browne's quote which I gave earlier. It is suggestive not only of the boundary condition between the Great Man Era and the Trait Theory Era, but of the essence of the paradigm shift. The excerpt follows:

> For approximately fifty years, and particularly during the past twenty-five years, psychologists and sociologists have been increasingly active in attempting to introduce the methods and knowledge of the human sciences into the study of leadership (Browne 1958).

---

[14] This is a moot point with modern day leadership theorists. For them, leaders are made not born. Bass(1981:29) argued that the Great Man versus environment which is a spin off of the "born or made" controversy is a pseudo-problem. For any given case, some of the variance in what happens is due to the situation, some is due to the individual, and some to the interaction of individual and situation. Thus, Mao Zedung played a critical role in the Chinese Revolution, but without the chaotic state of Chinese affairs under Kuomontang leadership his rise to power would not have been possible. Missiologists with theological presuppositions will want to look at the question afresh in terms of biblical examples of leaders chosen by God at birth.

[15] Frequently boundary conditions are clouded. See the Complexity Era. Some boundary conditions have explicit boundary events like the Stogdill (1948) paper during the boundary time between Trait and Behavior Eras. For unclear boundary times, it is only in retrospect that they can be analyzed as boundaries.

Around the turn of the century psychologists and sociologists increasingly began to study leadership. Their approach to leadership was more scientific and aimed at obtaining data and reflecting on that data. They did "scientific studies" to identify the qualities of Great Men that were fundamental to their leadership. One of the paradigm shifts that signaled a different era was that of a different methodology. It seems to me that as leadership study became more scientific, the biographical method[16] was less relied upon, and contrived laboratory experiments as well as field studies became more common. A second signal of a different paradigmatic era was the content being studied. It was characteristics of leaders and not the leaders themselves which were in focus. Also, the purpose of the research was clearer. Great Men just happened as a result of heredity and could be studied and admired. But trait theorists were suggesting that perhaps leaders could be made—that is, if common traits existed then perhaps some of them could be developed by training.

I must digress for a moment and point out the close connection between the issues of this boundary condition and my own present emphasis in leadership research. I am particularly interested in this paradigm shift between the Great Man Era and the Trait Theory Era since my own approach to leadership emergence patterns (called transformational life-history) is biographical in nature and hence identifies in spirit with the Great Man Era. Bear with me in the next several paragraphs as I pause to record some subjective, interpretive comments relating to my own research. This present paper is based on my findings in an earlier research tutorial (1986). Let me quote an observation from that work which points out an often seen characteristic of a boundary shift.

> One must recognize that as disciplines go through paradigm shifts there is a tendency to toss out the baby with the bath water—that is, old theories are discarded entirely (even though some of their findings are still relevant) as new ones come on the scene. One needs to appreciate what ought to be kept and

---

16 The idea apparently was that biographical information was highly subjective. Scientific analysis should be objective. However, Laudan (1977), Barbour (1974), Kuhn (1970) and other epistemological writers have demolished the myths of scientific objectivity. This myth still permeates the theological sciences. Worldview assumptions are rarely acknowledged as influencing findings. Findings are assumed to be objective.

utilized further as new ideas come on the scene. (Clinton 1986:23)

I feel that the biographical method which was primarily thrown out with the ascendance of Trait Theory over Great Man Theory needs to be examined again. As the field becomes more complex and takes into account macro-elements of leadership[17]—which is what I believe is being called for in the present Complexity Era—the biographical methodology will help leadership students see the correlation between contextual situations and development of individual leaders.

I was pleased to note that the biographical methodology has been resurrected from time to time. This affirms my own attempts at using it. One of my purposes in the leadership literature search was to find out if others had methodology of leadership research similar to my own. Further, I wanted to know if what I was doing was viable. I believe it is. The several references to it in different development phases seems to indicate that there is something of worth in the methodology. Bogardus noted its importance toward the end of the Trait Era (Bogardus 1934:11–13). Lloyd, during the middle of the Behavioral Era, attests to biographical methodology in training mid-career leaders from British management (Lloyd 1964). His methodology, though strictly secular, is not unlike my own in its intent and means of influencing the students. Urfick and Wolf (1984) in the Complexity Era were commissioned by the International Committee on Scientific Management (London) to study one hundred seventy pioneers in management history.

Bogardus' notion of "life-history" (Bogardus 1934:11–13) coupled with Burns' (1978:142) notion of "transformational leadership" can catapult biographical methodology relevantly into the Complexity Era and

---

[17] Macro-elements refer to elements outside the direct control of the organization itself: Societal pressures, international pressures, trends, Naisbitt's "megatrends," etc. These forces often have great impact on leadership within an organization, yet most leadership research looks narrowly within the organization for its variables of study. Yukl (1981) and Vroom and Yetton (1974) promote leadership theories broad enough to include macro-elements. From a biblical standpoint the sovereignty of God, divine guidance, providential call, etc. would lie in the domain of macro-elements that must be included in leadership study.

make it a fruitful research methodology especially appropriate for analysis of spiritual leadership.[18]

C. Termination of the Trait Phase—1948/Moving to Behavior Phase

The boundary between the Trait Era and the Behavioral Era is one of the clearest boundaries to spot since it was caused specifically by published material. Bass gives a footnote at the beginning of Chapter 4 which serves to clearly identify the termination of the Trait Era and signals the onset of the Behavioral Era.

> This chapter is a reprint of "Personal Factors Associated with Leadership: A Survey of the Literature," by Ralph M. Stogdill, which appeared in the **Journal of Psychology**, 1948, 25, 35–71. It is reprinted by permission of The Journal Press, Provincetown, Massachusetts. [This classic is included as it stands in this revised **Handbook of Leadership** since its publication marked the turning point in the study of leadership. Before this date, universal traits of leadership were emphasized. After the publication of this paper, specific situational analyses took over, in fact dominated the field, much more than argued for by Stogdill. As we will see, both individual traits and situational assessments as well as the interaction between them are important, and that was Stogdill's main thesis . . .] (Bass 1981:43)

Bass points out a series of influences which culminated in Stogdill's watershed research paper.

> In 1945, Shartle (1950b) organized the Ohio State Leadership studies. Shartle's background had been the study of job requirements and job performance. At that time nothing existed in the way of satisfactory leadership theory. Research before World War II had sought to identify the different traits of

---

[18] Stogdill has this to say in his watershed trait paper (Bass 1981:66) concerning this research methodology: "The most fruitful studies, from the point of view of understanding leadership, have been those in which leadership behavior was described and analyzed on the basis of direct observation or analysis of biographical and case history data."

leadership. However, analysis of this research by Bird (1940), W. O. Jenkins (1947), and Stogdill (1948; Chapter 4 of this Handbook) concluded that (1) little success had been attained in attempts to select leaders in terms of traits; (2) numerous traits differentiated leaders from followers; (3) traits demanded in a leader varied from one situation to another, and (4) the trait approach ignored the interaction between the leader and his or her group.

Since the personality trait approach was deemed to have proved fruitless, an attempt was made to study the behaviors rather than the traits of leaders—in other words, to describe individuals' behavior while they acted as leader of a group or organization. Hemphill (1949a) had already initiated such work at the University of Maryland. After joining the Ohio State Leadership Studies, Hemphill and his associates developed a list of approximately 1,800 items describing different aspects of leader behavior. The items were sorted by staff members into nine different categories or hypothetical subscales, with most items assigned to several subscales. However, staff members agreed that one hundred fifty items could be assigned to one subscale only. These items were used to develop the first form of the Leader Behavior Description Questionnaire—the LBDQ (Hemphill, 1950a; Hemphill & Coons, 1957).

Several factor-analytic studies by Halpin and Winer (1957) of item intercorrelations produced two factors identified by Hemphill as Consideration and Initiation of Structure in Interaction. Factor analysis of intercorrelations between the subscale scores also tended to yield two factors, and occasionally a third weak factor. The items and the subscales composed of the items measured two different patterns of behavior, rather than nine, as originally hypothesized. (Bass 1981:358)

And thus was born the Ohio State Leadership Theory which dealt with the two major leadership behavior factors, Consideration and Initiation of Structure in Interaction.[19] This theory was to dominate the leadership field for almost twenty years.

D. Termination of the Behavior Phase/Transition to Contingency Phase

The termination date of the behavior phase I identify with Fiedler's publication of **A Theory of Leadership Effectiveness.** In it Fiedler explained in detail his contingency model of leadership. Bass notes that, "Fiedler's (1967) contingency model of leadership is the most widely researched on leadership. At the same time, it is the most widely criticized" (Bass 1981:341). His model has been the dominant model from that time to this.

Fiedler is discussed more in detail in the section dealing with prominent personalities in the leadership field. But a brief mention of his background and what led to his contingency model is in order here. Fiedler's doctorate is in psychology. He began in the early 1950s to study the success of therapists as a function of their accuracy and assumed similarity to their patients. He extended this research to leaders and the effectiveness of the groups they led. Fiedler was concerned with leadership effectiveness and ways of measuring it and improving it. Eventually out of the refinement of tools he was using to gather input came the "Least Preferred Co-worker" tool, a controversial means for assessing a leader's attitude and orientation. The tool supposedly identifies primary orientation personality/style-wise toward task or relationship. A relatively high LPC score (favoring the least preferred co-worker) has most generally been conceived by Fiedler to be indicative of a relationship-motivated person, whereas a low LPC score (rejecting the least preferred co-worker) has been conceived to be indicative of a task-motivated person. Later in another section I will describe in more depth Fiedler's model. For now there are three things I want to point out:

1) It was this theory which radically shifted the focus of leadership study from behavioral analysis to leadership style

---

[19] Consideration refers to leadership behavior which is relationship-oriented. Initiation of structure refers to leadership behavior which is task-oriented. Often missionary leadership coming out of a western worldview is strongly task-oriented and operating in cultures which are relationship-oriented. See the Ohio State Research Model in Appendix B for further discussion on these two important leadership concepts.

analysis which also included variables beyond leadership behavior—followers and situation. This thematic focus which highlighted leadership research for ten to fifteen years paved the way for researching many other leadership variables, a trend typical of the fifth development phase—complexity.

2) The radical nature of Fiedler's theory is his methodology for increasing leader effectiveness which differs from most style theorists.[20] Bass points out the radical nature of Fiedler's remedial plan in the following quote:

Blake and Mouton (1964), Vroom and Yetton (1974), or R. Likert (1977a) would see the need to educate leaders to improve their styles. In the case of Blake and Mouton, it would be toward "9–9," the one best way. For Likert, it would be toward a democratic style. For Vroom and Yetton, it would depend on the problem situation. But Fiedler (1978) sees an entirely different course of action. Because a leader's LPC is what matters, and LPC is relatively unchanging, then either one must identify and select leaders of high or low LPC to fit given situations or leaders need to know their LPC scores and in what situations they are most effective in order to change the situation rather than themselves. Fiedler argues that changing leader-member's relations or task structure, or a leader's position power is easier than changing a leader's personality. (Bass 1981:357)

3) The theory is strongly dominated by a psychological theory of personality. Not all would agree with this underlying basis for the theory.[21]

---

[20] Fiedler differs from most style theorists. For Hersey and Blanchard (1977) styles can be learned. For Blake and Mouton (1964) styles flow from assumptions (worldview values) and can be changed. Blake and Mouton would be style theorists who hold to one ideal style while Hersey and Blanchard hold that various styles can be ideal depending upon situation characteristics and follower maturity.

[21] For example, Hersey comes at leadership from a behavioral psychologist's viewpoint and holds that while people generally have dominant styles they also have a style range. Even more important for Hersey is style adaptability. Hersey would hold that style range and adaptability can be influenced by training.

But Fiedler did move leadership further along in forcing it to identify and measure other variables and to point out the need to contribute theory which promotes effective leadership and seeks to measure it.

E. Transition To the Complexity Phase

I do not have a clear-cut boundary event for the ending of the contingency phase. But I noted that in the mid-seventies there have been numerous writings which are suggesting future trends that leadership research needs to address. There is a stream which originated with McGregor (1960), Maslow (1970), Levinson (1973), and more recently Maccoby (1978) which is concerned with motivational theory (which has at its roots philosophy and ethics). There is a stream broadly characterized as dealing with Organizational theory which began with Katz and Kahn (1966), and was increasingly focused on from differing perspectives by Likert (1969), Sells (1968), Greiner (1972), and Luthans (1975). This stream has pointed out the necessity of analyzing the broader context in which leadership emerges (a trend toward macro leadership elements). There is a stream, which was early signaled by Adorno et al in their research on authority, which has studied authority and power and its influence. Wrong (1980) shows how far this stream has come. The Carbondale Series (publications of the leadership conferences held at Southern Illinois University throughout the seventies) has reviewed leadership theory, stimulated new ideas, and in general pointed out how much more complex leadership is than models in the past had assumed. Writers like Greenleaf (1970, 1977) and Hodgkinson (1983) are pointing out the need for broader more comprehensive philosophical thinking to be injected into the leadership equation. These several streams along with the general dissatisfaction with the status quo of leadership research (seen in almost every recent review of leadership literature) leads me to believe that we are presently in a boundary phase—one in which the transition is not as clear cut as Stogdill and Fiedler's were.

III. DETAILED DISCUSSION OF DEVELOPMENT PHASES

Having identified the boundaries of each of the five major development phases, and having given enough information to flavor the character of each, I would now like to sweep through these periods once more from three perspectives. I will point out some of the more significant works in each phase, list the names of people who were prominent in each phase and give some examples of writings typical of the research and findings of the phase. I should point out that the significant works in a given era actually may not deal with the prominent theories of that era, but may reflect on a previous era or lay groundwork for theories in future eras.

A. Phase I. Great Man Era—1841–1904

Some prominent names for this era include Thomas Carlyle, F. Galton, William James, and F. A. Woods. Carlyle wrote his book in 1840. Galton did research from the late 60s till the 90s. James' observations come from the same period as Galton's. Woods wrote the results of his research in 1913. Though written in the Trait Era it was the culmination of thinking of the Great Man Era.

A typical work of this era would be Thomas Carlyle's **On Heroes and Hero-Worship**. It tended to reinforce the concept of the leader as a person endowed with unique qualities who was able to move the masses and inspire them.

Woods, James and Galton were prominent in influencing leadership theory. They did actual studies and drew observations from them. Galton's studies led him to focus on the hereditary background of great men. His findings were published in two books, **Hereditary Genius** in 1869 and **English Men of Science—Their Nature and Nurture** in 1890. James implied that the great changes in society were due to great men. Woods' research involved a historic study of fourteen nations over a period of several centuries. His book **The Influence of Monarchs** was published in 1913. His findings demonstrated that the conditions of each reign were found to approximate the ruler's capabilities (Bass 1981:27).

E. E. Jennings' book, **An Anatomy of Leadership: Princes, Heroes, and Supermen** published in 1960 gave a comprehensive review of Great Man theory. His subtitle points out his leadership typology which is explained by Bass.

Jennings (1960) subdivided these charismatic and strong patrimonial leaders differently. The great men and women who are rule breakers and value creators are supermen and women;

those who are dedicated to great and noble causes are heroes; and those who are motivated principally to dominate others are called princes. The princes may maximize the use of their raw power or they may be great manipulators. Heroes come in many varieties also: heroes of labor, consumption, and production, risk-taking heroes, and so on. Supermen may or may not seek the power to dominate others (Bass 1981:18).

One should remember not to judge the research efforts and leadership contributions of this era too harshly—that is, in the light of what is now known. Scientific methodology, in general, was in infancy. Published materials and availability of information were very limited. It was a beginning.

B. Phase II. Trait Era—1904-1948

Prominent people[22] in the Trait Era include Emory S. Bogardus and C. I. Barnard. Bogardus was one of the earliest social psychologists. In addition, he was interested in leadership. He is unusual in that he combines features of the Trait Theory Era along with features of the Great Man Era. I am particularly interested in Bogardus because of his interest in biographical methodology in studying leadership. His book, **Leaders and Leadership**, published in 1934,

... tackles the problem of leadership by analyzing leaders. If the immediate subject-matter of leadership is leaders, then the biographies, autobiographies, and other life records of leaders become the chief sources of pertinent data. While much in these

---

22 The selection of prominent people is not easy to determine due to selectivity biases of authors being studied. I am doing profiles on potential influentials. I have used two basic criteria to determine prominent people. One, in my general reading which includes scan, browse and ransack techniques of many articles and books, I look for evidence of innovators, facilitators, trend setters, researchers, applicators, and popularizers. A second criterion I used was the 33 page author index in Stogdill/Bass (1981) handbook. It lists each entry in the book where an author's name occurred. If an author is referred to enough times to have two lines of page numbers he is probably important. I marked all of these I could find then I looked them up by page number to see what was said. This enabled me not only to identify many more prominent people but gave me a method to evaluate systematically just how they had contributed. Appendix C lists the potential influentials list. Those marked with an asterisk (*) are entries for which I have already compiled detailed profiles.

accounts is chaff, yet kernels of revealing truth may be uncov-
ered in nearly all. A few are rich sources of the lore of leadership (Bogardus 1934:v).

He comments further on this approach.

The study of leadership may be pursued through the analysis of biographies, autobiographies, and "life histories." A great
deal may be expected of the case analysis method. Much of the
material in this volume has been secured in this way, and hence
the strong and weak points of the method may be presented
succinctly.

It is all too true that biographies and autobiographies are
weak in that they underestimate the importance of leadership as
a social process. They emphasize the role of the leader but not
of the led, of the individual but not of the group. The attitudes
and roles of the followers are largely overlooked. References
to these main considerations are often most superficial. A new
kind of autobiography of a leader is needed—one that will present the social situation, the social process, and the attitudes of
all concerned.

The nearest approach to meeting this need is the life history, but life history materials, so far, have usually been gathered
with the view to studying the nature of personal and social
disorganization. The way that was opened by Thomas and
Znaniecki promises well, although it has not been carried far as
yet. Life histories of leaders as well as of representative followers in the social situations in which the leaders have func-
tioned would be invaluable for the scientific study of leadership
(Ibid:11).

My own approach of "leadership emergence patterns" or "leadership
selection processes" resonates with this concept of "life history."

Another theorist of interest to me in particular is H. Person. Bass'
reference to him contained two important findings—both of which are
presuppositions in my own studies in leadership emergence patterns.

Person (1928) advanced two hypotheses to account for leadership: (1) any particular situation plays a large part in determin-

ing leadership qualities and the leader for that situation; and (2) the qualities in an individual which a particular situation may determine as leadership qualities are themselves the product of a succession of prior leadership situations which have developed and molded that individual (Bass 1981:28).

A second prominent person in this era is C. I. Barnard. Handy (1976:421) says of him that he is the most noteworthy of the prescriptive theorists from the Trait school. His book, **The Functions of the Executive** probably, along with Tead's works (1929, 1935), paved the way for management theory.

Bass cites several who are illustrative of researchers in this era.

If the leader is endowed with superior qualities that differentiate him from his followers, it should be possible to identify these qualities. This assumption gave rise to the trait theories of leadership. L. L. Bernard (1926), Bingham (1927), Tead (1929), and Kilbourne (1935) explained leadership in terms of traits of personality and character. Bird (1940) compiled a list of seventy-nine such traits from twenty psychologically oriented studies. A similar review was completed by Smith and Kruger (1933) for educators and by W. O. Jenkins (1947) for understanding military leadership (Bass 1981:27).

Stogdill's research paper, "Personal Factors Associated with Leadership: A Survey of the Literature," which was originally published in the **Journal of Psychology** in 1948, is probably the most famous work of this era. For two reasons it should be noted. One, it brought to an end the Trait Era simply because of the force of its findings.[23] Two, it was a thorough review of what Trait Theory had accomplished. It details findings, research methodologies, and many references to people and their work over the forty-plus years of trait research.

Another prominent work in this era occurred just after the date I used to end the era. It was the study, **The Authoritarian Personality**, by T. W. Adorno, E. Frenkel-Brunswik, D. J. Levinson and

---

23 Whether Stogdill's paper actually did this or not is not the point. It reflected the tenor of the dissatisfaction with Trait Theory research. It certainly vocalized publicly and widely the need for a paradigm shift.

R. N. Sanford.[24] This is one of the most famous leadership studies in the
history of leadership. It came as a response to the World War II Holocaust and was a reaction to authoritarian leaders like Hitler, Mussolini,
etc. It sought to analyze traits correlating to authoritarianism. It is significant for several reasons. One, it shows how a macro-context factor can
deeply influence and bring about change. Two, the book itself served as a
catalyst to temper strong leadership tendencies. I believe its findings
helped to swing the pendulum back toward democratic leadership.
McGregor, Likert and others followed in that trend and brought about a
focus on democratic leadership which carried through the sixties and into
the seventies. Handy makes an insightful comment on this trend when he
explains the popularity of some leadership theories in the sixties and
early seventies.

> Style theorists are best studied in their original works, e.g.
> Likert, McGregor, Blake and Mouton . . . . Although many
> of the style theorists pay lip service to the importance of the
> task and situational variables, they tend to be advocates or
> prophets of the participative culture. There is too little critical
> evaluation of when it works and when it does not—most of the
> studies are primarily concerned to establish that it is correlated
> overall with satisfaction or with productivity and are insensi-
> tive to explanatory conditions. The influence of some of these
> 'prophets' has been great but can, I think, be better explained
> on a cultural basis than on an efficiency criterion. They repre-
> sented a more democratic humanistic approach to the use of
> man in organizations and came at a time of reaction against sci-
> entific management (Handy 1976:422).

---

[24] This is an instance of macro context elements impacting on the entire leadership field.
Adorno et al (1950) had done their famous research on authoritarian personalities
(Hitler, Mussolini, etc.) as a reaction to World War II (Holocaust). There was a
mega-trend against authoritarian leadership. McGregor and others carried this macro-
contextual trend directly into the leadership field. They reacted against authoritarian
leadership and toward democratic/participative styles of management. This ramified
to theological education as well. See Wagner's **Leading Your Church to Grow**
(1984). Wagner recognized this trend and describes seminary thrusts in the sixties as
having produced facilitator-type leadership rather than strong leadership. He is writing in the throes of the counter-trend back to authoritarian leadership and thus advocates strong leadership to bring about church growth.

A third reason why this book is important is that it illustrates the importance of intervention time[25] in the change dynamics process. In boundary times between phases a timely idea can bring about change with rapidity and force.

C. Phase III. Behavior Era—1948–1967

While there were a number of prominent works that grew out of the dominant theory of the era, two which occurred were not directly involved with a study of consideration and initiating structure. These should be mentioned. In 1960 Douglas McGregor produced his book, **The Human Side of Enterprise.** He was an early harbinger of the style theorists who were to become increasingly popular toward the waning moments of the Ohio State theory. This book, or rather some of its motivational theory (theory x, theory y), is still widely used today.

A second important book came toward the end of the era. D. Katz and R. L. Kahn published **The Social Psychology of Organization** in 1966. This book is widely quoted in leadership literature and was innovative in its contribution to leadership studies in at least two ways. It showed the importance of macro-influences on leadership—that is, leadership takes place in a context which deeply influences the leadership. Secondly, it pointed out another important element in the leadership equation—organization. That is, it highlighted the importance of another whole stream of studies—those dealing with organizational analysis and development. This trend is seen further in Likert (1967), Sells (1968), Greiner (1972), Luthans (1975) and Adizes (1979).

Below are given some of the typical works of this era.

- Brown and Cohn's The Study of Leadership.

---

[25] In my ML563 Change Dynamics course I define several kinds of time which are important to change theory: historical context (local, regional, national), linear history (organizational), structural time (organizational), duration of change effort, intervention time, pace of change, and change track record. Pace of change time was referred to earlier in conjunction with Toffler's **Future Shock** (1970). Intervention time is the ripe moment to act when factors are such that the probability is high that change can most likely be accomplished. Intervention time is often a macro contextual variable and is illustrated in the biblical context by the case of John the Baptist (see Luke 3:1–2ff) and Paul's comments in Gal 4:4.

- Beer, Buckout, Horowitz, & Levy's "Some Perceived Properties of the Differences Between Leaders and Non-leaders."
- Likert's **New Patterns of Management** and **The Human Organization.**
- Bass' "Some Observations about a General Theory of Leadership."

Prominent people in this era include those who were working on the Ohio State leadership model, those who were forerunners of the contingency models, and those who advocated various stylistic theories. Concerning the Ohio State model, Stogdill, Shartle, and Hemphill set the pace. Bass, Fleishman and others spread the ideas to other centers of influence. Forerunners of the Contingency Model include Fiedler and those he was influencing. Influential style theorists included R. R. Blake and J. S. Mouton, R. Likert, and D. McGregor.

D. Phase IV. Contingency Era—1967–1980

Important and illustrative works during this era include many by Fiedler and his disciples. His book in 1967, **A Theory of Leadership Effectiveness,** summarized some fourteen years of his leadership research. His theory has generated more research than any other single theory in the history of leadership. Fiedler put his theory into a readable (popular language) programmed text (Wiley series) which sought to actually teach practitioners to use his theory.

Other important works include House's two articles in 1971, "A Path Goal Theory of Leader Effectiveness," which started another line of research and "A 1976 Theory of Charismatic Leadership" which is a theoretical attempt to update Weber.[26] The Path Goal theory of leadership is still a dominant approach to leadership research today.

---

[26] Weber's original research is almost classic. His three categories of sociological leadership role/types are still frequently referred to in leadership literature. Traditional leadership, legal leadership, and charismatic leadership were his three types. It was this third type, the charismatic, that House focused on in his article. He was able to bring to bear many new leadership perspectives in modifying Weber's concepts. Charismatic leadership is an important category seen frequently in church leadership.

Sell's chapter, "The Nature of Organizational Climate" in R. Tagiuri and G. L. Litwin's book **Organizational Climate: Explorations of a Concept**; Luthan's work, **Organizational Behavior**; and Handy's book, **Understanding Organizations**, were important contributions to the stream of leadership dealing with organizational theory. Adizes' article (1979), "Organizational Passages: Diagnosing and Treating Life-cycle Problems of Organizations," while more popular in format, contributed further to organizational theory by applying macro-analysis to organizations themselves. This stream of organizational theory is important to para-church and church leadership since both are social organizations, and "spiritual leaders" could benefit greatly from an understanding of the principles of organizational dynamics.

New theories, or at least substantially different aspects of contingency theories, were represented by several works. Hollander's book, **Leadership Dynamics: a Practical Guide to Effective Relationships**, put forth his "social exchange" theory of leadership and is a highly readable book. Hersey and Blanchard's **Management of Organizational Behavior** is for me a basal book which describes an aspect of contingency management other than Fiedler's. Their life cycle/situational approach to leadership is the theory I am most comfortable with of all the theories I have studied. The impact of their theory is yet to be felt, but will be, as Hersey is using "movement dynamics" to popularize this theory. He has created a graduate school of leadership and an organization for teaching his theory via workshops and seminars in industry. His workshops have trained several million practitioners. This kind of grass-roots movement will have impact on the entire field sooner or later. Yukl's research paper, "Toward a Behavioral Theory of Leadership," was a forerunner of his own leadership theory which was captured more fully in his book, **Leadership in Organizations**. Vroom and Yetton's **Leadership and Decision-Making** carries contingency theory further. They see the essence of leadership behavior wrapped up in decisions. Handy points out how they have expanded contingency theory.

> Vroom and Yetton have carried the contingency theories of leadership even further. They have looked at two aspects of a decision, its quality and the likelihood of its implementation, in terms of the nature of the task, the quality of the subordinates and their relationship to the leader. They have then produced a formal decision tree which minimizes the time taken for a

decision after consideration of these other factors. By making
the full contingency idea operational they have made it testable
and teachable. (Handy 1976:423)

Burns' work, **Leadership**, won a Pulitzer prize. It is different in
nature altogether from the leadership works I have been listing. It does
not have the perspective of psychology or sociology which dominate
much of leadership thinking. Burns is a philosophical historian with an
interest in leadership and historical leaders. His book is written in philosophical essay-like style. He is particularly interested in political leadership. His concept of "transformational leadership"[27] will probably be
influential as the philosophical element of leadership study gains promi-
nence in the Complexity Era.

The Carbondale Series (six different books which are compilations
of a national leadership conference held approximately every two years)
came out over a period of about eight years during the Contingency Era.
It is an important series since it looks back, capturing what has been done
in leadership studies, and looks forward pointing the way to new
research. I'll discuss this series more in Section IV.

In the area of motivational theory, several authors wrote important
books during the Contingency Era. Maslow's **Motivation and Personality**, Levinson's **The Great Jackass Fallacy**, and Maccoby's **The
Gamesman** deal with the motivational dimension of leadership—an element that will eventually spur leadership researchers to broaden leadership to include ethics and philosophy, a concept strongly advocated by
Hodgkinson.[28]

There are many prominent people in the Contingency Era. This is
especially so since toward the end of the era the complexity of leadership
is becoming increasingly evident. There are many specialties developing.
But if I were to narrow prominent people in the Contingency Era to

---

[27] His work along with Loye's (1977), **The Leadership Passion**, and
Hodgkinson's (1983), **Philosophy of Leadership**, put forth a compelling plea
for a return to philosophical/ideology as a major element in leadership. I think they
are indicative of a stream of thought which is becoming a major trend in the Complexity Era.

[28] I consider this to be so important that I give it as high a rank in leadership elements as
the leader basal elements and influence means. See Figure 8. I include in the philosophical element a theological component.

three, I would pick Fiedler, Hunt, and House—Fiedler because his contingency model has been the most dominant model in leadership history; Hunt because of his facilitator role in the Carbondale Series, and House because of his unique ability to think differently in an era dominated by situational leadership theory.

E. Phase V. Complexity Era—1980–?

Fiedler will be moving off the scene. My feeling is that House, Hersey, and Mintzberg will probably be prominent people in leadership in the initial phases of the Complexity Era. House has the ability to recruit people to do research along the line of theories he suggests. Hersey's leadership theory is one that speaks of complexity and is fluid, and takes into account so many of the diverse elements of leadership. And too, he will spread his theory at the grassroots level among practitioners. He will be influential. Mintzberg has clear goals.[29] He has set goals to learn as much about organizational theory as he can. Already he has produced four or more books by a major publisher. His leadership constructs also, like House, seem to attract researchers.

Whether or not Hodgkinson's book, **The Philosophy of Leadership**, will indeed become well known or influential, I cannot say. But I do think he is capturing a definite trend that will expand leadership studies beyond their "psychological captivity."[30]

---

[29] In my research of prominent influentials in the leadership field I researched in **Contemporary Authors in Print**. Each of the contemporary authors were personally interviewed on the phone. One questions repeated on all the interviews was, "What are your goals in leadership?" I was struck by Mintzberg's clear goals. His answer was to the effect that he intended to study and learn all he could about organizations in the next ten or so years. He has, in about five years since that remark, produced four major works on organizations, all printed by Prentice-Hall, all important works.

[30] Hodginson points out a Babylonian captivity of another sort.

Leadership, variously and however defined, has not gone unresearched. On the contrary it has, especially since the end of the last world war, become the object of intensive and extensive scrutiny. But a curious thing has happened along the way. There has developed a tendency to concentrate study under the rubric of psychology so that there has come about a certain specialization and monopolization; what we might call the **psychologizing of leadership**. Leadership thought is now a subdivision of psychology rather than of philosophy. What began in antiquity as a profoundly philosophical concern—how to find the guardian—has become demythologized, secularized, empiricized, democratized and psychologized, and

At the beginning of this paper I suggested that the broad aims of the paper would include:

1. identifying the paradigmatic eras,

2. recognizing some prominent people from each era,

3. noting some important written works of each era,

4. pointing out some of the centers of influence of leadership theory,

5. describing the dominant models of each era,

6. defining important leadership terms from this paradigmatic overview.

Sections I and II have focused on aims 1–3. The sections which follow will progress toward aims 4, 5, and 6.

IV. CENTERS OF INFLUENCE

Not only is it important to understand paradigmatic eras in leadership history, but it is also important to understand how the paradigms were spread. Centers of Influence refer to major institutions which influence change in the field. This section makes an initial attempt to identify some of these centers.[31] Though there are probably more centers of influence than the ones I have identified, I can at least say that the five I shall mention were influential.

Centers of influence are identified in several ways.

---

now flourishes as a thickly tangled web wherein notions of values, ethics and morality have been leached away, ignored, or deprecated as irrelevant (1983:197, 198). [Boldface emphasis my own.]

In like manner theology has been captured by philosophical paradigms and missiology by anthropology.

[31] I mentioned in Footnote 6 the limitations of selectivity. This area, noting of centers of influence, is one of the areas I was referring to which needs detailed research. Had I complete biographical profiles for all the prominent influentials listed in Appendix C, I would be able to do some comparative research following networks of influence and more correctly identify root centers of influence. As it is these five I list are centers of influence. Perhaps there are others which are more deserving of mention. Further research is needed.

1. They promulgate some model which dominates the field for a period of time.

2. They recruit many followers to do research concerning their models.

3. They produce literature about their model.

4. They facilitate information distribution by providing conferences or convocations to which prominent influentials in the field are invited.

5. They begin institutions which facilitate research and find ways to finance it.

6. They often bring about a major paradigm shift in the field with some of their innovative ideas.

7. They produce the texts that other leadership schools use.

I could not identify a center of influence in Phase I or II. But in Phase III, The Behavior Era, I noted at least three. These were Ohio State University, the Massachusetts Institute of Technology and the University of Michigan.

A. Ohio State University—A Center of Influence

At Ohio State were Stogdill, Shartle, and Hemphill. Their model of leadership focused on two major elements of leadership behavior— consideration and initiation of structure. This model dominated research for almost twenty years. This center of influence had as its prime drawing card the leading model of research of its day. It had an institute which was focusing on research. It produced students who went to other schools and became leading professors of leadership studies. One such early student of this influential center was Bernard Bass who himself became very influential at Louisiana State University and the State University of New York, Binghamton. In fact, his wide research experience, his connection with Ralph Stogdill, and his vast knowledge of the field as a whole led to his role of editing **Stogdill's Handbook of Leadership**. Because there is nothing even close to this book, Bass has become one of the most influential persons in the field of leadership. His selection of what to include, how to emphasize it, etc. is a tremendous illustration of the indirect power base. He will influence many leadership students since his

book is probably the only one that almost all leadership students will have
read.

B. Massachusetts Institute of Technology—A Center of Influence

I am least familiar with the center of influence at Massachusetts
Institute of Technology (MIT). Perhaps it is not really a center, but a single person—Douglas McGregor. However, I feel it should be mentioned
as there was tremendous macro-contextual pressure during the fifties to
move industrial leadership toward the democratic end (participative management) of the autocratic-democratic leadership style continuum. This
trend affected the philosophy of theological training and can be seen particularly in training which produced facilitator-type pastoral training in
the sixties.

McGregor had much to do with promoting this movement. His field
was industrial management. His book, **The Human Side of Enterprise,** broke ground since it questioned the assumptions that management
held about controlling its human resources. McGregor believed that
many of the assumptions underlying the management of people in the
1950s were far from adequate. He believed that assumptions held about
controlling human resources determine the whole character of the enterprise and the quality of successive generations of management. McGregor
was helped along the way by Alfred Sloan who both prompted research
and provided financial backing through the Alfred P. Sloan Foundation.[32]
This center of influence brought to the leadership field the questions of
how leaders motivate followers. It asserted philosophically that leaders'
views of followers will determine how leaders influence followers. This
motivational stream of study has continued to the present, though not primarily through MIT.

C. University of Michigan—A Center of Influence

A third center of influence was the University of Michigan. It carried out research at approximately the same time as the Ohio State Lead-

---

[32] This is another example of a macro-contextual variable. It points out the importance
of power (in this case financial) at a critical juncture (intervention time) which can
make the difference between the success or failure of a movement.

ership Studies. The focus of the Michigan research was identification of relationships among leader behavior, group processes and measures of group performance (Yukl 1981:113). A primary objective was to discover what pattern of leadership behavior leads to effective group performance. Likert (1961), in his book entitled **New Patterns of Management**, attempted to integrate the findings of the Michigan studies and provide a theoretical framework to explain them. Yukl (1981:115) summarizes four major elements highlighted by Likert as a result of the University of Michigan studies: Supportive Behavior, Group Method of Supervision, High-Performance Goals, and Linking Pin Functions. In his explanation of his Causal Relationship Model, Likert described three kinds of variables: causal variables, intervening variables and end-result variables.[33] See Yukl (1981:116–117) for a brief explanation of the variables and the causal processes. Bowers and Seashore also proposed a theory, called the Four Factor Theory, to explain managerial effectiveness in terms of four categories. Their theory was based on a reconceptualization of the findings in the early Michigan studies and the Ohio State studies. Yukl (1981:118) describes the four factors. The labels for the four factors are support, interaction facilitation, goal emphasis, and work facilitation.

D. University of Washington—A Center of Influence

A fourth center of influence was the University of Washington, the location of Fred Fiedler. It became a center of influence during the last part of the Behavior Era and throughout the Contingency Era. Fiedler has been able to recruit the largest research following of any single leadership influential. He has been able to define research projects, find people to do them, find the way to finance them and convince the many groups that were to participate in them to allow them to take place. His 1979 article with Linda Mahar is a typical illustration of this ability to bring about research. The article, entitled "A Field Experiment Validating Contingency Model Leadership Training," occurs in **The Journal of Applied Psychology**, 1979a, 64, 247–254. I was reading this article

---

[33] These variables are now common place terms used in almost all the major models of the Complexity Era. The major models of the Complexity Era like Yukl's (1981) and Vroom-Yetton (1974) are framework models which have generic higher level categories than the more empirically focused models of the contingency. Likert's concepts take on more importance in such high level generic models.

at the University of California at Irvine when it dawned upon me just how much was involved in pulling together this one research project, which is probably typical of hundreds he has done. This was a field experiment in which ROTC cadets (both men and women) were given contingency training (self-study) prior to summer camp. Analysis of commissioned and non-commissioned officer evaluations of performance, as well as peer ratings, showed that the one hundred fifty-five male and thirty-five female cadets with LEADER MATCH training performed better than the one hundred seventy-six male and thirty-nine female cadets in the control group. The ROTC cadets came from numerous universities. I was a NROTC cadet. I went to summer camps. Sometimes there were fifty or more schools represented at these summer camps. So I appreciated the amount of coordination that had to go on to get permission for the cadets to be involved, get them to do the self-study package, and to get the cooperation of the Army summer camps. In any case, it is evident that Fiedler is a person of immense energy and influence. He is a strong leader and somewhat confrontational as he has taken a lot of flack in the journals. But no one can doubt that his work has made the University of Washington the most influential center of influence for leadership over the past twenty years.

E. Southern Illinois University—A Center of Influence

A fifth center of influence has been Southern Illinois University. This has been a different kind of influence. Southern Illinois University has hosted a major leadership conference several times for over a decade. Outstanding leadership influentials have participated. Theory papers have been presented and critiqued. Instrumental in facilitating this affair have been James G. Hunt and L. L. Larson. This center of influence has produced what I call the Carbondale Series—a series of volumes documenting the presentations and findings of the various conferences. Much reflection on what has gone on in leadership theory, stimulation as to what ought to be going on, and the setting of future research trends has taken place because of this center of influence. I list the Carbondale Series in "References Cited in This Paper." See the six entries co-authored by Hunt.

V. THE DOMINANT MODELS AND THEORIES IDENTIFIED

In this section I shall mention the dominant models I have identified throughout the five paradigmatic eras. My intent is not to define the model fully here, but simply to place it in its historic context and describe it very generally. Appendix B, using an information mapping[34] technique, defines these models in terms of some of their underlying assumptions and various essential characteristics.

A. Great Man Theory

At the beginning of the twentieth century, leaders were regarded as superior individuals who could be differentiated from the masses—or followers—whom they led to accomplish great things or to impact the flow of history of the human race. They could be differentiated from the followers on the basis of qualities which they had as a result of fortunate inheritance and/or which were brought out or developed by social situations at moments of destiny. The study of leadership at this time was restricted primarily to the study of personal leaders who had somehow demonstrated these qualities and uniquely shaped history. The research approach method was a popularized biographical and philosophical reflection method.

I describe Great Man Theory as an approach to leadership which focuses on identifying leaders who have impacted significantly the course of human history and which describes philosophically general principles of leadership observed in the lives and actions of these leaders.

Three important assumptions underlie the model:

1. History has been shaped by the leadership of great men.

2. The study of this leadership primarily focuses on why these leaders emerged. Two basic theories include:

   a) Hereditary Theory,

   b) Social Stimulus Theory.

3. Lessons can be generalized which may be helpful.

---

[34] Information mapping is a system of writing which is designed for auto-didactic materials preparation. Robert E. Horn of Information Systems Inc. authored the system.

The basic idea of hereditary theory is that leaders are superior people because they are endowed with superior qualities which differentiate them from followers. The central idea of the social theory is that the emergence of a great leader is a result of stimuli: time, place, and circumstance.

The Great Man Theory served as a stepping stone to the Trait Theories of the early 1900s. The natural bridge to Trait Theory followed this assumption: "If the leader is endowed with superior qualities that differentiate him from his followers, it should be possible to identify these qualities."

B. Early Trait Theory

At the close of the Great Man Era, the beginning of the twentieth century, leaders were regarded as superior individuals who could be differentiated from the masses, or followers, whom they led to accomplish great things. The leadership research of the next several decades sought to prove how they could be differentiated from the followers on the basis of qualities which they possessed.

I describe Early Trait Theory as a research paradigm which sought to explain leadership as directly related to superior qualities possessed by leaders.

Three important assumptions include:

1. Some persons are "natural leaders." That is, they are endowed with certain traits not possessed by others.

2. Empirical research should be able to distinguish the traits of leaders from those of followers.

3. Those possessing leadership traits will emerge as leaders.

Trait research was facilitated by the rapid development of psychological testing during the period from 1920 to 1950.

Early Trait Theory, which had dominated leadership research for nearly fifty years was unceremoniously dumped as the major research paradigm after Stogdill's (1948) major review. However, it did continue as a minor paradigm, called Latter Trait Theory, throughout the next two paradigmatic eras.

C. Latter Trait Theory

Following the publishing of Stogdill's article on Trait Theory the general mass of leadership researchers pulled away from Trait Theory and went into Behavior Theory. One group of researchers continued Trait Theory research with generally good results. This group, industrial psychologists, were interested in improving managerial selection. They were studying leaders who were working in relatively similar situations with relatively similar follower characteristics. A major emphasis of their study was to focus on the relation of leader traits to leader effectiveness, rather than on the comparison of leaders and nonleaders (Yukl 1981:69).

I describe Latter Trait Theory as leadership research efforts which sought to explain leadership effectiveness in management and administrative roles by relating effectiveness to traits.

Some basic assumptions underlying this research approach include:

1. Persons who consistently lead effectively will possess certain traits.

2. Empirical research should be able to relate leader traits to effectiveness.

3. Predictions about who will be effective leaders can be made by utilizing measures which identify the traits identified in the empirical research.

In the research by Latter Trait theorists, a greater variety of measurement procedures were used (Yukl 1981:69). Research methodology was becoming much more sophisticated. Projection tests such as the "Thematic Apperception Tests" and the "Miner Sentence Completion Scales" were used. Situational Tests such as the "In-Basket" and the "Leaderless Group Discussion" helped pinpoint the selection of emergent leaders. Forced Choice tests such as "Ghiselli's Self-Description Inventory" and "Gordon's Survey of Interpersonal Values" were used as means of identifying and selecting managerial types with potential for success. Yukl (1981), in his section on Trait Theory, pages 67–91, describes these issues in much more detail and gives references for further research.

Latter Trait Theory, with its intentional focus on traits associated with successful behavior, has potential for missiological application. Can traits of successful church planters be identified? Where situational and follower variables are relatively constant, the focus on leader traits can most likely be correlated to influence variables and power variables. Findings could prove valuable in church-planter selection processes.

D. Ohio State Leadership Research Model

Fleishman (1973:3), in reviewing the Behavior Era, describes what was happening: "The shift in emphasis during that period was from thinking about leadership in terms of traits that someone 'has' to the conceptualization of leadership as a form of activity that certain individuals may engage in." Shartle, Hemphill, Carter, Nixon and Stogdill were catalysts in bringing this shift. Researchers first generated a list of about 1800 statements of supervisory behaviors which were reduced to ten general categories. Halpin and Winer (1952), utilizing factor analysis, reduced the categories to two major and two minor, which eventually resulted in the two major factors, consideration and initiating structure.

I describe the Ohio State Leadership Research Model as a research model which uses questionnaires to measure leadership behavior under two major categories—consideration and initiating structure—and correlates this behavior to various efficiency criteria relating to attainment of group goals.

Four assumptions underlying this approach include:

1. Generally, various acts of leadership behavior can be grouped under two major categories—one called "consideration" and the other called "initiating structure."

2. Behaviors representing these two categories can be measured using various questionnaires (three primarily: LBDQ, SBDQ, LOQ)

3. The two are independent dimensions of leadership behavior.

4. Combinations of these patterns will correlate consistently to various effectiveness criteria.

The factor analysis study by Halpin and Winter (1952) paved the way for assumption 1. Assumption 3 was a breakthrough in the Ohio State research of leader behavior.

Consideration involves leader behaviors indicating friendship, mutual trust, respect, warmth, rapport between leader and follower, leader supportiveness, representation of subordinate interest, openness of communication, etc.

Initiating structure involves leader behaviors indicating concern with directing subordinates, clarifying of roles, establishment of well defined patterns and channels of communication and ways of getting job done, problem solving, criticizing poor work, pressuring subordinates to perform better, planning, coordinating, etc.

Leader effectiveness was usually measured by the task performance of the leader's work unit, but other supplementary criteria include satisfaction with the leader and negative follower behavior such as grievances, absenteeism, turnover.

E. Contingency Models

Stogdill's watershed article (1948) forced a paradigm shift from a direct focus on study of leaders (Great Man and Trait theories) to what leaders do—their behavioral functions. The Ohio State and Michigan studies reduced leadership behavior to two basic generic categories—consideration and initiation of structure. How leaders did these two basic functions became the focus of the next period of leadership research. Leadership style was the topic which described the fundamental ways leaders operated. At the heart of all contingency theory lies the concept of leadership styles. Figure 6 seeks to categorize contingency models in terms of style assumptions.

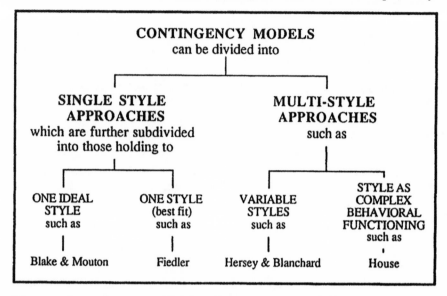

Figure 6. Advocates of Various Contingency Models in Terms of Style Approach

Table 1 Summarizes several theorists, their contingency models, and the basic issues involved.

Theorist	Model	Basic Issue Involved
Blake & Mouton	Managerial Grid	The ideal leadership style is very high in relationship and very high in task. All leaders should strive for this style.
Fiedler	Contingency	A leader's style is related basically to his/her personality and thus can not be changed easily. Hence, one must either adjust the situation to fit that dominant style or change the leader to a situation for which his/her style functions best.
Hersey & Blanchard	Situational	Style is a function not only of situation but also of follower maturity. Different styles are optimally related to different follower maturity levels. A leader can be trained to use a multi-style which fits situation and follower maturity.
House	Path-Goal	Style is contingent on means of influencing toward goals

Table 1. Comparison of Style Theorists

Models which see leadership as a dynamic process involving leaders, followers, leader-follower relationships, task, and other situational variables fall into the category called contingency models. The first model which actually went by this name was Fiedler's Contingency Model, but the concept of leadership as a process which is contingent on more than just the leader, his traits or his personality was broader than just Fiedler's Model.

Blake and Mouton had devised a model, called the Managerial Grid, as early as the mid-fifties which indicated that leadership effectiveness was directly proportional to a best leadership-style which integrated a high task focus with a high relationship focus. Fiedler and others held that leaders had styles which were directly a function of personality and hence could not be altered easily. Therefore, for Fiedler effective leadership was contingent on discovering a leader's style and matching it to situational variables in which that style was most effective. Hersey and Blanchard, like Blake and Mouton, believed that leaders could be trained to utilize different styles, but unlike them saw various styles as optimally related to various combinations of follower and situational variables.

I define a "Contingency Model" as the label describing leadership theories which see leadership effectiveness as contingent upon leadership styles, followers and situational variables.

The most famous of the contingency models is Fiedler's. Fiedler's Contingency Model sees effectiveness (where effectiveness is primarily performance toward organizational goals) as a function of matching one of two leadership styles (task-oriented or relations-oriented) with two kinds of general situations (favorable and unfavorable). Situational favorableness depends on three variables: leader-member relations, task structure and position power. Task-oriented leaders perform more effectively in very favorable and very unfavorable situations, while relations-oriented leaders perform more effectively in situations intermediate in favorableness.

F. Blake And Mouton's Managerial Grid

In the mid-1960s Blake and Mouton published their book, **The Managerial Grid**. In it is a diagram called "The Managerial Grid" which is a display along an x-y axis. The y axis describes "concern for people". It is scaled from 1 (low concern for people) to 9 (high concern for people). The x axis describes "concern for production." It is scaled from 1 (low concern for production) to 9 (high concern). While not being exactly the same, these two variables are closely related to "consideration" and "initiating of structure" of the Ohio State model and "task" and "relations" of Fiedler's model. On the diagram are plotted five basic orientations that a leader could have to express how concern for production and concern for people are joined. Mouton and Blake make it clear that though people seem to be predisposed to manage in one way or another, the points on the grid are not to be thought of as personality types that isolate a given individual's behavior. Identification on the grid does not slot a person in a rigid and inflexible way. Behavior is flexible and can be changed.

I describe the Managerial Grid as a leadership theory which relates the integration of concern for production with concern for people into five basic clusters, each having basic assumptions which will influence leadership style. It advocates the high concern for people and the high concern for task cluster as the optimum leadership style for effectiveness.

Mouton and Blake asserted that managerial effectiveness in organizations is optimum when using a leadership style representing the 9,9 plot.

Some key assumptions of Blake and Mouton include:

1. A given individual's style may be viewed as flowing from a dominant set of assumptions, though there are backup assumptions which also influence the style.

2. These assumptions orient the leader as to thinking and behavior in handling production/people relationships.

3. Whenever a person's underlying managerial assumptions change, actual managerial practices also normally shift.

4. Any leader can accept new assumptions and change behavior accordingly.

5. A style, even a dominant one, is not fixed but varies as affected by the following elements: organization, situation, values, personality, chance.

6. Many styles are subject to modification via training.

G. Fiedler's Contingency Model

Though I have already briefly described Fiedler's model when I illustrated the general definition of contingency models, let me give it further special attention. The leadership theory which has been most dominant throughout leadership history in terms of generating discussion and research has been Fiedler's Contingency Model. It is one of the earliest and certainly best known of the situational theories of leadership.

Fiedler, a psychologist by background, did early research which basically tried to predict leader effectiveness using a measure of leader attitudes called the LPC (least preferred co-worker). Essentially this was a trait approach to leadership. When he found different results for different kinds of leaders, he developed a contingency theory to explain the discrepancies. The model predicts that high LPC leaders, those with a motivational bias toward close interpersonal relationships, including subordinates, will perform more successfully in situations intermediate in favorableness. Low LPC leaders, with a bias toward achieving tasks, perform more successfully in very favorable and very unfavorable situations.

I describe Fiedler's Contingency Model as a leadership model which predicts effectiveness based on a leader's basic personality orientation toward achievement of task or relationships with followers and the leadership situation.

One strength of Fiedler's model is its strong assertiveness on predicting whether or not a given leader will produce well in a given situation. His predictions can be summarized as follows.

1. Low (task-oriented) LPC leaders perform better and run more effective groups when there is either very high or very low situational control (that is, the quality of leader-member relationships, the degree of task structure, and the position power of the leader are either altogether highly favorable or altogether highly unfavorable to the leader).

2. High (relations-oriented) LPC leaders are most effective when there is intermediate situational control.

I describe nine assumptions underlying this model. See Fiedler's Contingency Model in Appendix B. Of the nine, the key assumption for me is assumption 3: "A leader's style is a function of his/her personality and is basically fixed and falls dominantly into one of two styles (task-oriented or relationship-oriented)." It seems to me that this assumption, while generally true, can be challenged by findings of "transformational life-history" and by careful longitudinal study of leadership styles of biblical characters.[35]

---

[35] Doohan's (1984) analysis of Paul's leadership as perceived in Thessalonians, Galatians, Corinthians, Romans, and Phillippians is a step in the right direction. Her final conclusions of Paul and his leadership show a strong inclination towards Hersey and Blanchard's situational approach to leadership and a tendency to use Hollander's transactional concepts also.

H. Hollander's Exchange Theory

Hollander, in a brief historical reflection, places his own theory as different from but developing parallel (in time) to contingency theories.

The lack of generalizability of the trait approach led to two interrelated developments. First was the description of leader behavior, in varying organizational roles. Second, was the situational approach, which emphasized the characteristics of the particular situation and task in which the leaders were mutually involved. The stress was on the demands made for particular leader characteristics.

An extension of the situational approach was the development of contingency models. These models attempted to specify what leader attributes are appropriate, given certain contingencies in the situation. They emphasized factors calling forth different leader qualities to achieve effectiveness.

A parallel development in time was the transactional approach, which considered the quality of the relationship between the leader and followers. The perceptions by followers of the leader's status and legitimacy are significant to this concept (Hollander 1978:45).

Hollander's theory is basically a transactional one which fuses the situational approach to leadership and the social exchange view of interpersonal relationships. I describe it more formally as a theory which approaches the study of leadership as a social process of influence involving an on-going transaction between a leader and followers, and has its locus in the overlap between three basal elements (leader, situation, and followers).

Hollander focuses on the relationship between leader and followers. Legitimacy, authority, status, and bases of influence are key concepts in Hollander's view of leadership. Some essentials of his model include:

1. Leadership is primarily a process, not a person.
2. Leadership structure provides a framework for the process.
3. The process of leadership involves a social exchange between the leader and followers in a situation.

4. Leaders provide certain benefits to the followers.

5. Followers provide certain support essentials to the leader.

6. The followers' perceptions of the leader's actions and motives are central to a transactional approach.

7. Leadership is a mutual activity in which there usually is both influence and counter-influence.

8. Ability to exert influence is the major operational quality of authority and depends upon transactional processes.

I. Hersey And Blanchard's Situational Model

Another contingency model, one which moves more toward complexity models, is Hersey and Blanchard's model. Hersey and Blanchard predict that the more managers adapt their style of leader behavior to meet the particular situation and the needs of their followers, the more effective they will tend to be in reaching personal and organizational goals. They define style as ". . . the behavior pattern that a person exhibits when attempting to influence the activities of others as perceived by those others" (Hersey & Blanchard 1982:95–96). A second quote gives their views on leader's abilities to have different styles and no one best style—issues on which they differ with Fiedler and Mouton/Blake. "In summary, empirical studies tend to show that there is no normative (best) style of leadership. Effective leaders adapt their leader behavior to meet the needs of their followers and the particular environment. If their followers are different, they must be treated differently. Therefore, effectiveness depends on the leader, the follower(s), and other situational variables; $E = f (l,f,s)$. Therefore, anyone who is interested in his or her own success as a leader must give serious thought to these behavioral and environmental considerations" (1982:103).

I describe their situational model as a multi-style leadership model which advocates that as leaders vary styles and appropriate power bases according to follower maturity, effectiveness increases. Their model necessitates a focus on the evaluation of followers and the development of followers. Their model is complex and is based on an interplay among (1) the amount of guidance and direction (task behavior) a leader gives; (2) the amount of socio-emotional support (relationship behavior) a leader provides; and (3) the readiness (maturity) level that followers exhibit in performing a specific task, function or objective.

J. House's Path-Goal Leadership Model

Bass (1981:444) traces path-goal theory back to research done by Georgopoulos, Mahoney, and Jones in 1957. The theory was popularized by M. G. Evans and Robert J. House. House's paper, "A Path-Goal Theory of Leader Effectiveness" in 1971, formalized the model to include situational variables and gave it a wide hearing. The Path-Goal Model is founded on motivational theory (expectancy theory). I describe it as a situational leadership theory that asserts leadership behavior (a causal variable) acts to influence subordinate expectancies and valences (intervening variables) to bring about subordinate effort and satisfaction (end-result variables) and is moderated by characteristics of task and subordinates (situational moderator variables). Notice the use of Likert's terminology referred to earlier. House's model like Hersey and Blanchard's, is a model on the boundary between contingency models and complex models. This is a detailed model and must be studied in depth for a proper understanding. See Yukl (1981:144–153) and House (1971) for more detail.

K. Vroom-Yetton Normative Decision Making Leadership Model

The normative focus of this model is seen in their assumptions in the following quote.

> We set out to examine leader behavior both normatively and descriptively. The two questions, "How should leaders behave if they are to be effective?" and "How do they behave?" have been in the background of all of the work presented in the previous nine chapters. Since one cannot effectively examine all aspects of leader behavior simultaneously, we chose one aspect that, on the basis of previous work, was likely to be of major importance. We selected the leader's role in the decision-making process ... (Vroom & Yetton 1973:197).

I describe the Vroom-Yetton leadership research framework model as a model which seeks to evaluate leadership study under five major

elements: personal attributes, leader behavior, organizational effectiveness and two types of situational variables. Schematically the model is
diagrammed as shown in Figure 7.

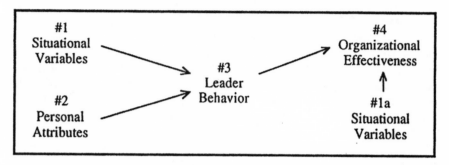

Figure 7. Vroom-Yetton Normative Model

The key variable (or set of variables) in the figure is labeled #3,
Leader Behavior—the actions or behaviors exhibited by the leader in the
course of carrying out his/her leadership role. The decision process used
by the leader is one (and only one) of the variables that might be used in
the analysis of such behavior. With respect to #1 and #2, Leadership
Behavior is the dependent variable and is studied using descriptive
methodology. With respect to #4, Leader Behavior and #1a, Situational
Variables are independent variables and #4 Organizational Effectiveness
is the dependent variable. The interrelation of these variables is studied
using normative methodology.

L. Yukl's Multiple Linkage Leadership Model

Yukl, in order to provide a more comprehensive theory of leadership which took into account situational moderator variables and intervening variables at the same time, posited his Multiple Linkage Model in
1971. It has since been modified to include a larger number of intervening variables and to include a wider range of more specific leadership
behaviors. In addition to a leader's short-term influence on the intervening variables, the model also recognizes the leader's longer term capacity
to modify situational variables as a means of improving group performance (Yukl 1981:153).

I describe Yukl's Multi-linkage Model as a situational leadership model which sees leadership behavior (a causal variable) acting immediately to influence intervening variables (six given) and acting long term to change situational variables (three different categories distinguished) in order to bring about subordinate performance.

As is the case with House's model and Hersey and Blanchard's and Vroom-Yetton's model, this is a model which advances the concept of contingency into the Complexity Era. See Appendix B where this model is defined schematically. Yukl's assumptions are worth noting:

1. A leader's effectiveness in the short run depends on the extent to which he/she acts skillfully to correct any deficiencies in the intervening variables for his/her work unit.

2. The situation determines which intervening variables are most important, which ones are in need of improvement, and what potential corrective actions are available to the leader.

3. Over a longer time period, leaders can act to change some of the situational variables and create a more favorable situation.

VI. SOME FINAL OBSERVATIONS—THE LEADERSHIP EQUATION

I want to close this paper by noting some observations, some of which I have mentioned in passing and now want to clarify and emphasize.

A. Eight Observations

1) *The locus of leadership (that is, the content of that which has been focused on and researched) has gone through a major paradigm shift.*

The time-line can be divided into two large portions broken by the major paradigm shift stimulated by Stogdill's paper (Figure 2). If you were to title these, the first would be called "Leaders," the second, "Leadership." An analysis of the overall time-line of the history of leadership studies sees that the five phases can be broken up into two larger portions. Phases I and II focus on the study of leaders while Phases III, IV, and V expand from the study of leaders to leadership. Hollander and Julian in reviewing leadership (up to the year 1969) make a comment which confirms this observation.

> An early element of confusion in the study of **leadership** was the failure to distinguish it as a process from the **leader** as a person who occupies a central role in that process. Leadership constitutes as an influence relationship between two, or usually more persons, who depend upon one another for the attainment of certain mutual goals within a group situation. This situation not only involves the task but also comprises the group's size, structure, resources, and history, among other variables. (Hollander & Julian 1969:388)

   2) *The research methodology has gone through several major changes.*

Methodology from psychology and sociology has dominated leadership research. As techniques in statistics and research methodology have become increasingly more sophisticated, so too has leadership research methodology.[36] Hodgkinson gives a helpful but too-brief analysis of the research picture.

> The sequence of exploratory research has been, in the general line of its logic, from maxims or rules of thumb through Trait Theory, to Factor Analytic Trait Theory (yielding the classical two dimensions of task orientation and person orientation), to situational qualifications, to interactive considerations (task plus leader plus followers plus interactions) to the latter-day refined maxims of path-goal analysis and to the current complexities of Professor Fiedler's work (Hodgkinson 1983:198).

   3) *Leadership is a complex process embracing several elements.*

I find that one of the most helpful insights for me that has come out of this paradigmatic analysis is the need for balance and an overall per-

---

[36] What are needed are some new research paradigms for leadership. I am interested in Glaser and Strauss' (1967) Grounded Theory approach. McCall (1976) and Greene (1977) are suggestive along these lines.

spective or framework to view the complexity of leadership. As models move from the simplistic Great Man Theory to the High Level Generic Models of the Complexity Era one can see the addition of leadership variables. From a study of the five development phases and a recognition of how each new phase added some new element to the study of leadership, I have categorized the streams of leadership under three major headings and six sub-categories as shown in Figure 8.

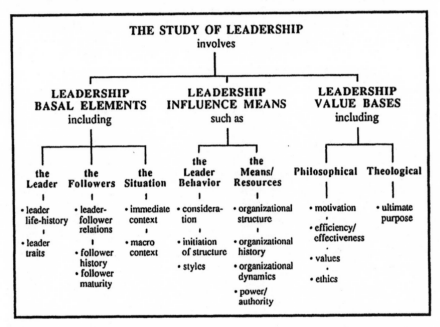

Figure 8.   Hierarchical Categories Relating Total Leadership Elements

I will use this framework in my Section B to define the leadership equation. It is a helpful framework for analyzing research paradigms for balance and completeness. It is also a helpful framework for organizing bibliographic leadership materials.[37]

---

[37] See my paper, "Reading In the Illusive Field of Leadership," which uses this framework to provide the backdrop for the organization of thirteen mini bibliographies on

4) *Leadership is becoming a multi-disciplinary field which has a history of paradigm shifts not unlike the field of anthropology.*

A comparison of Langness' (1974) work and this paper confirms this observation.

5) *Each new phase adds a complexity to the concept of leadership.*

This could be graphically demonstrated if I were to build up Figure 8 step by step as I went through each phase similar to the way I developed the paradigmatic time-line. For example, the Great Man Era would have had only the left-most path of Figure 8 and only the sub-element leader life-history.

6) *Leadership will by necessity remain a multi-disciplined field of study.*

I say this for several reasons. Presently various aspects of leadership are taught in so many departments involved[38] in so many different universities with vested interests that it does not seem likely that any one kind of department will ever dominate the leadership field. I believe that leadership is a rich concept which affects many aspects of life. Various disciplines which study life will view leadership through perspectives which will uniquely contribute to the whole synergistically. This is a helpful thing. However, what is needed is some integrating core course(s) which all leadership students must study.

7) *The Complexity Era is pointing out the necessity of including macro-influences.*

The later high level generic models in the Complexity Era recognize the limitations of narrow research. Research methodologies must somehow be found which can embrace these wider variables.

---

leadership. (1) Leadership Theory, (2) Leadership History, (3) Leadership Philosophy, (4) Leadership Transformational Life-History, (5) Leadership Trait Theory, (6) Leadership Contingency Models, (7) Leadership Follower Element, (8) Leadership Christian Perspectives, (9) Leadership Power, (10) Leadership Organizational Dynamics, (11) Leadership Change Dynamics, (12) Leadership Styles, (13) Leadership Research.

[38] I listed some twenty-four different kinds of departments in footnote 2. And I am fairly certain that I have not exhausted them.

8) *A paradigmatic overview helps prevent the natural built-in
tendency in a paradigm shift to discard old theories entirely
(even though some of their findings are still relevant).*

Old paradigms should be reviewed continually to see if they can be
adapted by later findings to bring fresh insights. I believe transformational life-history is doing just that.

There have been gains in the leadership field, even though basically
most of them are in the direction of finding out how much more we don't
know about leadership. Phase I was more philosophical and broader in its
approach toward a theory of leadership. Phases II, III, and IV have been
narrow, utilizing empirical research in micro-situations. Phase V promises to move again toward a broader approach to leadership. I will include
here an overall chart, Table 2, which updates the simple time-line of
Figure 5 by adding other categories for comparison. This chart suggests
a movement toward more complexity in the latter eras.

	I → Great Man	II → Trait	← III → Behavior	← IV → Contingency	← V → Complexity
	1841 1904		1948	1967	1980 1986
boundary conditions	Psychological Sociological entry into leadership		Stodgill's research paper	Fielder's book	plethora of publications dealing with complexity of leadership elements
methodology	biographical	sociometry empirical exper. field exper. statistics	increasingly behavioral science methodology questionnaires e.g. LBDQ factor analysis	same as III more toward micro/ empirical questionnaires e.g. LPC	same as III trend toward macro/
focus on	leader	leader attributes	leader behavior	leadership styles; situational elements of leadership	organizational culture & other larger macro elements of leadership
end result	principles rule of thumb	lists of qualities	measurements of behavior functions such as initiation, consideration	measurements of style correlated to other elements	? my guess toward two extremes: pragmatic; philosophical applications
dominant theory	Great Man Theory	Trait Theory	Ohio State Leadership Theory	Fiedler's Contingency Model; Other Situational theories: Hollander; Hersey & Blanchard; House, Path-Goal	no one will dominate; multiple theories

Table 2.   Time-Line Overview of Leadership History

B. Expanding My Definition of Leader

I have attempted in this paper to develop a paradigmatic overview of leadership. Such a framework provides an overall context for examining leadership. It is in this overall framework that various definitions in the leadership field should be scrutinized. Figure 8 is helpful in this regard. In this final section I want to review my definition of a leader and propose several new generic-like definitions that may prove helpful in maintaining balance and avoiding the tendency to mold definitions to fit needs.[39]

I was able to use the categories of Figure 8 to examine anew my definition of a leader. I hope the following discussion will illustrate what I mean when I say a paradigmatic overview brings balance. I have been utilizing the following definition[40] of a leader prior to my paradigmatic overview study.

A leader, in the biblical context, is a person,

- with God-given capacity AND
- with God-given responsibility

TO INFLUENCE

- a specific group of God's people
- toward God's purposes for the group.

I feel comfortable with that definition. However, I have expanded my understanding of each component of the definition through the broadening process that has occurred in doing this paradigmatic research. In each of the descriptions emphasizing my expansion of understanding, you will need to refer to Figure 8.

---

[39] Stogdill, in describing motivations behind definition formulations, serves to warn us of the tendency to use definitions for our own purposes. "Definitions vary with purposes they serve. Investigators have developed definitions to serve the following purposes: (1) identify the object to be observed, (2) identify a form of practice, (3) satisfy a particular value orientation, (4) avoid a particular orientation or implication for practice (5) provide a basis for theory development." Bass (1981:15). Thus it is helpful to examine definitions in light of a broad framework like this paradigmatic overview.

[40] My definition of leader flowed from my studies of individual leaders in the Old Testament and from a study of numerous leadership passages in the New Testament such as: Acts 20:17–38, I Peter 5:1–11, I Thessalonians 5:12, 13, Hebrews 13:7, 8, 17.

My view of capacity has now been enlarged by my understanding of Trait Theory and motivational patterns of a leader by the studies of the Behavioral Era and Contingency Era. It already included giftedness, natural abilities and functional skills.

My view of responsibility which included accountability to God for results of leadership and burden for a ministry has been expanded by the third major leadership element—leadership philosophy/theology which has subsections of efficiency/effectiveness, values and ethics.

My view of a specific group of God's people focuses on the major leadership element of followers. In studying the contingency theories and especially Hersey and Blanchard and related offspring research like Moore's (1976) Follower Maturity, I have come to a new appreciation for follower maturity in terms of which style and power base a leader should be using. Leadership style theory in general has made me aware more than ever before of the crucial interplay between leader and follower. Previously I knew the importance of assessing spiritual gifts and spiritual maturity of the followers. Now I have added the whole concept of skills maturity and psychological maturity along with my previous view of followers. The subcategories under FOLLOWERS, leader-follower relations, follower history, and follower maturity all have helped me focus on this third component of my definition.

My view of the fourth component, toward God's purposes for the group, has been broadened by a look at several subcategories:

- under SITUATION,
    immediate context
    macro-context
- under MEANS/RESOURCES,
    organizational structure
    organizational history
    organizational dynamics
- under LEADERSHIP PHILOSOPHY
    motivation (both leader and follower foci)
    effectiveness
    values (both leader and follower foci)
    ethics.

The fourth component, God's purposes, also does much to shed light on secular theory in terms of the whole leadership element of LEADER-SHIP THEOLOGY/PHILOSOPHY and especially on the macro-context subcategory under the leadership element, SITUATION.

My view of INFLUENCE in the definition, the central thrust of the definition, has been greatly widened by my study of the subcategories of the leader element LEADER BEHAVIOR. I was also strengthened by my cursory study into the subcategory, power/authority, under the leader element, MEANS/RESOURCES.

C. Some Definitions: Leader Act, Leadership, The Leadership Equation

In broadening my leadership locus beyond primarily a leader locus I have been forced to define the broader concept, leadership, within which my leader definition fits. I have used the tree diagram of Figure 8 as a basis for formulating my working definition. Of special interest is the concept of persistence over time. I have noted the concept of a leadership act which recognizes the broad idea of influence and allows for any person at a given moment to be seen as a leader (LePeau 1983:10). But leadership in my thinking deals with persistence of leadership acts over time. This certainly is in line with examples of biblical leadership.

A *leadership act* is the specific instance at a given point in time of the leadership influence process between a given leader (person influencing) and follower (person or persons being influenced).

Leadership is

(1) a dynamic process over an extended period of time in various situations

(2) in which a leader utilizing leadership resources,

(3) and by specific leadership behaviors,

(4) influences the thoughts and activity of followers,

(5) toward accomplishment of person/task aims,

(6) mutually beneficent for leaders, followers and the macro-context of which they are a part.

I have then symbolized this working definition as follows as a further attempt to help me integrate the complex concepts involved in leadership.

The leadership equation is based on the shortened form of leadership definition. *Leadership* is the integration over time of leadership basal elements as processed with leadership influence means and evaluated for consistency with leadership philosophy.

symbolic formula $\quad L = \int_{T_1}^{T_2} \dfrac{[L_b] \, \Delta \, [L_m]}{[L_p]}$

where L = leadership considered as a whole

where $\displaystyle\int_{T_1}^{T_2}$ = the process of integrating variables over time

where L_b = leadership basal elements made up of leader, follower, situation aspects

where Δ = as processed with

where L_m = leadership influence means made of up of leader behavior and leader power aspects

where —— = as evaluated for consistency with

where L_p = leadership philosophical/theological elements (ethics, directiveness, motivational philosophy of self and group)

A step forward then is to look at leadership effectiveness as a measure of leadership in terms of consistency with some leadership criterion. This criterion presently varies greatly in the leadership field. In the Christian view of leadership, effectiveness will have to include the major macro-context item of God's purposes and means for accomplishing his purposes. But in general the symbolic shorthand notation for viewing leadership effectiveness is as follows.

$$L_{eff} = \frac{L}{E_c}$$

where L_{eff} = leadership effectiveness

where E_c = effectiveness criteria

It is my concern that our own efforts at studying leadership both through missiologically and theologically informed perspectives have some sort of impact on this "psychologizing of leadership." I realize this will have to be a long-range concern, but if God is indeed pointing out the necessity of a leadership stream being added to missiological thought then we should set some long range goals toward providing rigorous research and credible leadership models which can impact secular leadership theory. For the short range my concern is getting a leadership emphasis into Missiology, but I am also thinking long range.

I introduce this leadership equation as a means for examining any given research model to see if the model is balanced. It is also useful in doing comparative studies of leadership across cultures.[41]

CLOSURE

This paper's intent was to overview the history of leadership theory from the mid-1800s until 1986 with an aim toward:

1. identifying the paradigmatic eras,

2. recognizing some prominent people from each era,

3. noting some important written works of each era,

4. pointing out some of the centers of influence of leadership theory,

5. describing the dominant models of each era,

6. defining important leadership terms from this paradigmatic overview.

All of these aims have been touched upon. The ultimate intent was to ground leadership students in the field of leadership so as to prepare

---

[41] I intend to demonstrate this in a future paper. I will use the leadership equation in a similar manner to Vroom and Yetton's (1974) use of their framework model.

them for advanced studies in leadership. Being well grounded means one should

1. be familiar with the overview of history of the field,

2. know the prominent people who have influenced the discipline,

3. be at least familiar with and perhaps, further, know the prominent ideas, models and theories of the field,

4. know the kind of leadership research that has been done and the trends toward future research,

5. be able to use perspectives from this overview to analyze leadership situations in other cultural situations.

This paper has provided help on items 1–3. Items 4 and 5 will be the focus of advanced studies.

References Cited in Paper

Adizes, Ichak
　　1979　　"Organizational Passages: Diagnosing and Treating Life-cycle Problems of Organizations" in **Organizational Dynamics**. Volume 8, No. 1, Summer, pp. 2–25.

Adorno, T. W., Frenkel-Brunswik, E., Levinson, D. J., & Sanford, R. N.
　　1950　　**The Authoritarian Personality**, New York: Harper.

Ashour, A. S.
　　1973　　"The Contingency Model of Leadership Effectiveness: An Evaluation." in **Organizational Behavior and Human Performance**. Vol 9, pp. 339–355.

Barbour, Ian G.
　　1974　　**Myths, Models, and Paradigms**. New York: Harper & Row.

Bass, B. M.
　　1981　　**Stogdill's Handbook of Leadership**. New York: The Free Press.

Beer, M., Buckhout, R., Horowitz, M. W., & Levy, S.
　　1959　　"Some Perceived Properties of the Differences between Leaders and Non-leaders" in **Journal of Psychology**. Vol. 47, pp. 49–56.

Bernard, L. L.
　　1926　　**An Introduction To Social Psychology**. New York: Holt.

Bingham, W. V.
1927   "Leadership" in **The Psychological Foundations of Management.** (H. C. Metcalf, ed.) New York: Shaw.

Bird, C.
1940   **Social Psychology.** New York: Appleton-Century.

Bogardus, Emory S.
1934   **Leaders and Leadership.** New York: Appleton-Century.

Browne, C. G. & Cohn, T. S.
1958   **The Study of Leadership.** Danville, IL: Interstate.

Burns, J. M.
1978   **Leadership.** New York: Harper & Row.

Carlyle, Thomas
1963 (1907) **On Heroes and Hero-Worship.** New York: Doubleday.

Clinton, J. Robert
1984   **Leadership Emergence Patterns.** Altadena: Barnabas Resources.

Clinton, J. Robert
1986   Reading in the Illusive Field of Leadership (to be published).

Clinton, J. Robert
1986   "Reflections on a Leadership Bibliographic Search." (Unpublished doctoral paper.) Pasadena: School of World Mission, Fuller Theological Seminary.

Clinton, J. Robert
1986, 1992 **Coming To Some Conclusions on Leadership Styles.** Altadena: Barnabas Publishers.

Doohan, Helen
1984   **Leadership in Paul.** Wilmington, Delaware: Michael Glazier, Inc.

Fiedler, F. E.
   1967   **A Theory of Leadership Effectiveness.** New York:
             McGraw-Hill.

Fleishman, E. A.
   1973   "Twenty Years of Consideration and Structure" in **Cur-
             rent Developments in the Study of Leadership.**
             (E. A. Fleishman & J. G. Hunt, Eds.) Carbondale:
             Southern Illinois University Press.

Galton, Sir Francis
   1890   **English Men of Science: Their Nature and Nur-
             ture.** New York: Appleton, Century.

Greene, C. N.
   1977   Disenchantment with Leadership Research: Some Causes,
             Recommendations, and Alternative Directions. In J. G.
             Hunt & L. L. Larson (Eds.), **Leadership: The Cut-
             ting Edge.** Carbondale: Southern Illinois University
             Press.

Greenleaf, Robert K.
   1970, 1973 **The Servant As Religious Leader.** Peterborough,
             N.H.: Center for Applied Studies.

Greenleaf, Robert K.
   1977   **Servant Leadership.** New York: Paulist Press.

Greiner, Larry E.
   1972   "Evolution and Revolution as Organizations Grow" in
             Harvard Business Review, July–August 1972,
             pp. 37–46.

Halpin, A. W., & Winer, B. J.
   1957   "A Factorial Study of the Leader Behavior Descriptions"
             in **Leader Behavior: Its Description and Mea-
             surement.** (R. M. Stogdill and A. E. Coons, eds.)
             Columbus: Ohio Sate University, Bureau of Business
             Research.

Handy, Charles B.
1976, 1981   **Understanding Organizations**. Second Edition.
             London: Penguin Books.

Hemphill, J. K.
1949   "The Leader and His Group" in **Journal of Educa-
             tional Research**. Vol. 28, pps. 225–229, 245–246.

Hemphill, J. K.
1950   "Leader Behavior Description" (mimeograph paper).
             Columbus: Ohio State University, Personnel Research
             Board.

Hemphill, J. K. and Coons, A. E.
1957   "Development of the Leader Behavior Description Ques-
             tionnaire" in **Leader Behavior: Its Descriptions
             and Measurement**. (R. M. Stogdill and A. E. Coons,
             eds.) Columbus: Ohio State University, Bureau of Busi-
             ness Research.

Hersey, P., & Blanchard, K. H.
1977   **Management of Organizational Behavior**.
             Englewood Cliffs, N.J.: Prentice-Hall.

Hodgkinson, Christopher
1983   **The Philosophy of Leadership**. New York: St.
             Martin's Press.

Hollander, E. P.
1978   **Leadership Dynamics: a Practical Guide to
             Effective Relationships**. New York: Free Press.

House, R. J.
1971   "A Path-Goal Theory of Leader Effectiveness" in
             Administrative Science Quarterly. Vol. 16, pps.
             321–338.

House, R. J.
    1977   "A 1976 Theory of Charismatic Leadership" in **Leadership: The Cutting Edge.** (J. G. Hunt & L. L. Larson, eds.), Carbondale: Southern Illinois University Press.

Hunt, J. G. & Larson, L. L. (eds.)
    1979   **Crosscurrents in Leadership.** (S. Ill. Leadership Symposium Series) Carbondale: S. Ill. U. Press.

Hunt, J. G. , & Larson, L. L.
    1977   **Leadership: the Cutting Edge.** Carbondale: Southern Illinois University Press.

Hunt, J. G., & Fleishman, E. A.
    1973   **Current Developments in the Story of Leadership.** Carbondale: Southern Illinois University Press.

Hunt, J. G., & Larson, L. L. (Eds.)
    1974   **Contingency Approaches to Leadership.** Carbondale: Southern Illinois University Press.

Hunt, J. G., Sekaran, U., & Schriesheim, C. A. (Eds.),
    1981   **Leadership: Beyond Establishment Views.** Carbondale: Southern Illinois University Press.

Hunt, J. G., & Larson, L. L.
    1975   **Leadership Frontiers.** Kent, Oh: Kent State University Press.

Hutcheson, Richard G. Jr.
    1979   **Wheel Within The Wheel—Confronting the Management Crisis of the Pluralistic Church.** Atlanta: John Knox Press.

James, W.
    1880   "Great Men, Great Thoughts and Their Environment" in **Atlantic Monthly,** Vol. 46, pps. 441–459.

Jenkins, W. O.
1947   "A Review of Leadership studies with Particular Reference to Military Problems" in **Psychology Bulletin**. Vol. 44, pps. 54–79.

Jennings, E. E.
1960   **An Anatomy of Leadership: Princes, Heroes, and Supermen**. New York: Harper.

Katz, D. & Kahn, R. L.
1966   **The Social Psychology of Organization**. New York: Wiley.

Keating, Charles J.
1982   **The Leadership Book**. Paulist Press.

Kilbourne, C. E.
1935   "The Elements of Leadership" in **Journal Coast Artillery**. Vol. 78, pps. 437–439.

Knowles, Malcolm S.
1984   **Andragogy in Action: Applying Modern Principles of Adult Learning**. San Francisco: Josey-Bass.

Kraft, Charles H.
1977   **Christianity in Culture**. New York: Orbis.

Kuhn, Thomas
1970   **The Structure of Scientific Revolutions**. 2nd Edition. Chicago: University of Chicago Press.

Langness, L. L.
1974   **The Study of Culture**. San Francisco: Chandler and Sharp

Laudan, Larry
1977   **Progress and Its Problems—Toward a Theory of Scientific Growth**. Berkley: University of California Press.

Le Peau, Andrew T.
1983   Paths of Leadership. Downers Grove, Ill.: InterVarsity Press.

Levinson, Harry
1973   The Great Jackass Fallacy. Cambridge: Harvard Univ. Press.

Likert, R.
1967   The Human Organization. New York: McGraw-Hill.

Likert, R.
1961   New Patterns of Management. New York: McGraw-Hill.

Lloyd, Humphrey
1964   Biography in Management Studies. New York: Humanities Press.

Loye, D.
1977   The Leadership Passion. San Francisco: Jossey-Bass.

Luthans, Fred and Kreitner, Robert
1975   Organizational Behavior Modification. New York: McGraw-Hill.

Maccoby, M.
1978   The Gamesman. New York: Bantam Books.

Machiavelli, N.
1940   The Prince. New York: Modern Library.

Maslow, Abraham
1970   Motivation and Personality. New York: Harper & Row. Second Edition.

McCall, M. W., Jr.
1976   "Leadership Research: Choosing Gods and Devils on the Run" in Journal of Occupational Psychology. Vol. 49, pps. 139–153.

McCall, M. W., Jr., & Lombardo, M. M. (Eds.),
    1978   **Leadership: Where Else Can We Go?** Durham, N.C.: Duke University Press.

McDonough, Reginald M.
    1979   **Keys To Effective Motivation.** Nashville: Broadman Press.

McGregor, Douglas
    1960   **The Human Side of Enterprise.** New York: McGraw-Hill Book Company.

Moore, Loren I.
    1975   Towards the Determination of Follower Maturity: An Operationalization of Life Cycle Leadership. Unpublished Doctoral Dissertation.

Person, H.
    1928   "Leadership as a Response to Environment" in **The Educational Record: Educational Record Supplement.** No. 6, pps. 9, 10–21.

Powers, Bruce F.
    1979   **Christian Leadership.** Nashville: Broadman Press.

Schaller, Lyle
    1971   **The Change Agent.** Nashville: Abingdon.

Sells, S. B.
    1968   "The Nature of Organizational Climate" in **Organizational Climate: Explorations of a Concept.** (R. Tagiuri and G. L. Litwin, eds.), Cambridge, Mass.: Harvard University Press.

Shartle, C. L.
    1950   "Studies of Leadership by Interdisciplinary Methods" in **Leadership in American Education.** (A. G. Grace, ed.), Chicago: University of Chicago Press.

Shawchuck, Norman
    1981   How to Be a More Effective Church Leader.
                Downers Grove, IL: Spiritual Growth Resources.

Smith, H. L., & Krueger, L. M.
    1933   A Brief Summary of Literature on Leadership.
                Bloomington: Indiana University School of Education
                Bulletin.

Stogdill, Ralph Melvin
    1948   "Personal Factors Associated With Leadership: A Survey
                of the literature" in Journal of Psychology, pps. 25,
                35–71. Also occurs as Chapter 4 "Leadership Traits:
                1904–1947" in Stogdill's Handbook of Leadership:
                A Survey of Theory and Research, (revised and
                expanded edition by Bernard M. Bass).

Tead, O.
    1935   The Art of Leadership. New York: McGraw-Hill.

Tead, O.
    1929   The Technique of Creative Leadership. In Human
                Nature And Management. New York: McGraw-Hill.

Toffler, Alvin
    1970   Future Shock. New York:

Urfick, Lyndall F., Wolf, William B.
    1984   The Golden Book of Management: A Historical
                Record of the Life and Work of More than One
                Hundred Pioneers. London: International Committee
                on Scientific Management.

Urfick, Lyndall F., Wolf, William B.
    1984   The Golden Book of Management: A Historical
                Record of the Life and Work of Seventy Pio-
                neers. London: International Committee on Scientific
                Management.

Vroom, Victor H., & Yetton, Phil W.
1974   **Leadership and Decision-making.** New York: Wiley.

Wagner, C. Peter
1984   **Leading Your Church to Growth.** Ventura: Regal.

Weber, M.
1946   "The Sociology of Charismatic Authority" in **From Max Weber: Essays in Sociology.** (H. H. Mills and C. W. Mills, eds. & translators), New York: Oxford University Press.

Wood, James R.
1981   **Leadership in Voluntary Organizations—The Controversy over Social Action in Protestant Churches.** New Brunswick: Rutgers University Press.

Woods, F. A.
1913   **The Influence of Monarchs.** New York: Macmillan.

Wrong, Dennis H.
1980   **Power—Its Forms, Bases and Uses.** New York: Harper & Row.

Yukl, Gary A.
1971   "Toward a Behavioral Theory of Leadership" in **Organizational Behavior and Human Performance.** Vol. 6, pps. 414–440.

Yukl, Gary A.
1981   **Leadership in Organizations.** Englewood Cliffs, N.J.: Prentice-Hall.

Appendix A.

Leadership Bibliography—Historical Overview

by Dr. J. Robert Clinton
School of World Mission
Fuller Theological Seminary
Pasadena, California
2 May 1986

LEADERSHIP BIBLIOGRAPHY—HISTORICAL OVERVIEW

Historically from a paradigmatic viewpoint modern leadership research and theory breaks down into five phases: Phase I. Great Man Era: 1841–1904; Phase II. Trait Era: 1904–1948; Phase III. Behavior Era: 1948–1967; Phase IV. Contingency Era: 1967–1980; Phase V. Complexity Era: 1980–present. I recommend that you first read my paper giving the overview of leadership history. Then you will have a framework in which to integrate any of the materials in a given phase.

Overall

Clinton, J. R.
1986   A Paradigmatic Overview of the Leadership Field From 1841–1986. Pasadena: School of World Mission, unpublished doctoral paper.

Comments: This surveys the leadership field from the mid-1850s to the present. It identifies the major boundaries between paradigms, identifies dominant models for each phase, prominent works for each phase, and prominent influentials, as well as defines 11 important models or theories during this historical period.

Great Man Era: 1841–1904

Jennings, E. E.
1960   **An Anatomy of Leadership: Princes, Heroes, and Supermen.** New York: Harper.

Comments: A review of the Great Man Era with interpretive analysis.

Early Trait Era: 1904–1948

Stogdill, Ralph Melvin
    1948   "Personal Factors Associated With Leadership: A Survey of the Literature" in **Journal of Psychology**, pps. 25, 35–71. Also occurs as Chapter 4 "Leadership Traits: 1904–1947" in **Stogdill's Handbook of Leadership: A Survey of Theory and Research**, (revised and expanded edition by Bernard M. Bass).

Comments: This watershed work terminated most of trait research (Latter Trait Theory is the exception). The locus of leadership was drastically affected by this boundary work. The leadership locus prior to this time was primarily leaders; after this time it was the basal elements of leadership: leader, follower, situation and influence means.

Latter Trait Era: 1948–1970

Bass, B. M.
    1981   "Traits of Leadership: A Follow-up to 1970," Chapter 5 in **Stogdill's Handbook of Leadership**. New York: The Free Press.

Comments: Gives the details of leadership trait research for the period.

Yukl, Gary A.
    1981   "Leadership Traits and Skills," Chapter 4 in **Leadership in Organizations**. Englewood Cliffs, N.J.: Prentice-Hall.

Comments: Yukl makes the insightful comment that Trait Theory during this period of time was seeking to identify traits of leaders who were functioning successfully. That is, it correlated leader traits with successful leadership behavior. Early Leadership Trait Theory tried to differentiate traits of leaders from traits of followers. Earlier Trait Theory omitted situation and follower variables while Latter Trait Theory accounted for them.

Behavioral Era: 1948–1967

Fleishman, E. A.
  1973   "Twenty Years of Consideration and Structure" in **Current Developments in the Study of Leadership.** (E. A. Fleishman & J. G. Hunt, eds.) Carbondale: Southern Illinois University Press.

Comments: The paradigm shift from traits to leadership behavior is described by one who was there.

Contingency Era: 1967–1977

Yukl, Gary A.
  1981   Section entitled "Fiedler's Contingency Model of Leadership" in **Leadership in Organizations.** Englewood Cliffs, N.J.: Prentice-Hall. pps. 132–139.

Comments: Gives a readable explanation of Fiedler's model, the dominant model of this era.

Fiedler, F. E.
  1972   "How Do You Make Leaders More Effective?" in **Organizational Dynamics,** Vol 1, No. 2, Autumn, p. 3–18.

Comments: Catches the flavor of Fiedler in a less technical format than most of his research articles.

Mitchell, T. R. et al
  1970   The Contingency model in **Academy of Management Journal,** 13.

Comments: Again, this is seeking to give a short summary of Fiedler.

Complexity Era: 1977–Present

Yukl, Gary A.
  1981   "Overview and Integration," Chapter 10 in **Leadership in Organizations.** Englewood Cliffs, N.J.: Prentice-Hall.

Comments: Note Figure 10–1 which is an attempt to integrate the complex variables in leadership research.

Hersey, P., & Blanchard, K. H.
      1977   **Management of Organizational Behavior.**
                    Englewood Cliffs, N.J.: Prentice-Hall.

Comments: This book presents Hersey and Blanchard's Situational model, illustrative of the Contingency Era. It clearly defines concepts and clarifies issues. Its multiple-style perspective sees leadership style and power base as being primarily a function of situation and follower maturity. It differentiates success from effectiveness.

Appendix B.

Eleven Models And Related Concepts

GREAT MAN THEORY—PRE 1900s LEADERSHIP
APPROACHES
Time Period: 1840–1900

introduction

At the beginning of the twentieth century leaders were regarded as superior individuals who could be differentiated from the masses, or followers, whom they led to accomplish great things or to impact on the flow of history of the human race. They could be differentiated from followers on the basis of their qualities which resulted from fortunate inheritance and/or which were brought out or developed by social situations at ripe moments of destiny. The study of leadership at this time was restricted primarily to the study of personal leaders who had somehow demonstrated these qualities and uniquely shaped history. The research approach method was a popularized biographical and philosophical reflection method.

description

The *Great Man Theory* describes an approach to leadership which focuses on identifying leaders who have impacted significantly on the course of human history, and which writes philosophically in terms of general principles of leadership observed in the life and actions of these leaders.

assumptions

1. History has been shaped by the leadership of great men.
2. The study of this leadership primarily focuses on why these leaders emerged. Two basic theories included:
   a) Hereditary Theory, b) Social Stimulus Theory
3. Lessons can be generalized, which may be helpful.

Basic idea: leaders are superior people because they are hereditary
                   theory endowed with superior qualities which differenti-
                   ate them from followers.

CONTRIBUTORS: F. Galton, F. A. Woods, A. E. Wiggam

Basic idea: The emergence of a great leader is a result of social
                   stimulus, time, place, and circumstance.

CONTRIBUTORS: S. Hook, E. Mumford, E. S. Bogardus, H. S. Person

uses   The Great Man Theory served as a stepping stone to the
                   Trait Theories of the early 1900s. The natural bridge to
                   Trait Theory followed this assumption: "If the leader is
                   endowed with superior qualities that differentiate him
                   from his followers, it should be possible to identify these
                   qualities."

example   Bogardus represented one who bridged the Great Man
                   Theory and Trait Theory. This quote from his preface
                   illustrates the assumptions of Great Man Theory and
                   links it to Trait Theory.

                   "The research upon which this book is based has resulted
                   in two major sets of observations: one relating to the
                   origins of leadership, the other to the principles of
                   leadership. The origins, which have been located in three
                   main human centers—heredity, social stimuli, and
                   particularly personality traits-are illustrated by new and
                   fresh materials. The more penetrating of the
                   biographical and autobiographical materials that have
                   been used seem to justify a tentative presentation of
                   several leadership principles." (Bogardus 1934:v)

EARLY TRAIT THEORY
Time Period: 1904–1948

introduction

At the beginning of the twentieth century leaders were regarded as superior individuals who could be differentiated from the masses, or followers, whom they led to accomplish great things. The leadership research of the next several decades sought to prove how they could be differentiated from the followers on the basis of qualities which they possessed.

description

Early Trait Theory refers to the leadership research efforts which sought to explain leadership as directly related to superior qualities possessed by leaders.

assumptions

1. Some persons are "natural leaders." That is, they are endowed with certain traits not possessed by others.
2. Empirical research should be able to distinguish the traits of leaders from those of followers.
3. Those possessing leadership traits will emerge as leaders.

comment

Trait research was facilitated by the rapid development of psychological testing during the period from 1920 to 1950.

kinds of

Yukl (1981) identifies three categories of traits studied most traits frequently in the early trait period.

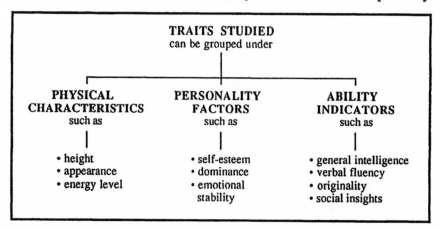

comment   Excerpts from Stogdill's basic conclusion on the Trait
           Era show a balance still important today. "A person does
           not become a leader by virtue of the possession of some
           combination of traits, but the pattern of personal charac-
           teristics of the leader must bear some relevant relation-
           ship to the characteristics, activities, and goals of the fol-
           lowers. Thus, leadership must be conceived in terms of
           the interaction of variables which are in constant flux
           and change. The factor of change is especially character-
           istic of the situation . . . . The personal characteristics
           of the leader and of the followers are, in comparison,
           highly stable. It becomes clear that an adequate analysis
           of leadership involves not only a study of leaders, but
           also of situations (Bass 1981:66–67).

Further study   See Yukl (1981:67–91); Bass (1981:43–72).

LATTER TRAIT THEORY

Time Period: 1949–1970

introduction
Following the publishing of Stogdill's article on Trait Theory the general mass of leadership researchers pulled away from Trait Theory and went into Behavior Theory. One group of researchers continued Trait Theory research with generally good results. This group, industrial psychologists, were interested in improving managerial selection. They were studying leaders who were working in relatively similar situations with relatively similar follower characteristics. A major emphasis of their study was to focus on the relation of leader traits to leader effectiveness, rather than on the comparison of leaders and nonleaders (Yukl 1981:69).

description
Latter Trait Theory refers to the leadership research efforts which sought to explain leadership effectiveness in management and administrative roles by relating effectiveness to traits.

assumptions
1. Persons who consistently lead effectively will possess certain traits.
2. Empirical research should be able to relate leader traits to effectiveness.
3. Predictions about who will be effective leaders can be made by utilizing measures which identify the traits identified in the empirical research.

comment
In the research by Latter Trait Theorists, a greater variety of measurement procedures was used (Yukl 1981:69).

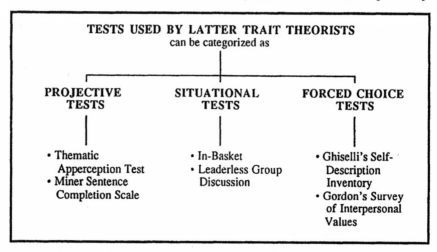

use   Findings from research on leader traits and skills have
               the greatest potential application to the selection and pro-
               motion of managers and administrators in large organi-
               zations (Yukl 1981:89). Three uses of Latter Trait Theo-
               ry include:
               •   the generating of information for making predictions
                   about likely success in a higher managerial position,
               •   the identification of training needs,
               •   long term career planning.
contributors   Miner, McClelland, England, Gordon
Further study See Yukl (1981:67–91); Bass (1981:73–96).

OHIO STATE LEADERSHIP RESEARCH MODEL
Time Period: 1950–1973

introduction
Fleishman (1973:3) in reviewing the Behavior Era describes what was happening in these words. "The shift in emphasis during that period was from thinking about leadership in terms of traits that someone 'has' to the conceptualization of leadership as a form of activity that certain individuals may engage in." Shartle, Hemphill, Carter, Nixon and Stogdill were catalysts in bringing this shift. Researchers first generated a list of about 1800 statements of supervisory behaviors which were reduced to ten general categories. Halpin and Winer (1952), utilizing factor analysis, reduced the categories to two major and two minor, which eventually resulted in the two major factors: consideration and initiating structure.

description
The *Ohio State Leadership Research Model* is a research model which measures leadership behavior using questionnaires and correlates this behavior under two major categories—consideration and initiating structure, to various efficiency criteria relating to the attainment of group goals.

assumptions
1. Generally, various acts of leadership behavior can be grouped under two major categories—one called consideration and the other called initiating structure.
2. Behaviors representing these categories can be measured using questionnaires (three primarily: LBDQ, SBDQ, LOQ).
3. The two are independent dimensions of leadership behavior.
4. Combinations of these patterns will correlate consistently to various effectiveness criteria.

comment   Consideration involves leader behavior indicating con-
               sider-friendship, mutual trust, respect, warmth, rapport
               between a tion leader and follower, leader supportive-
               ness, representation of subordinate interest, openness of
               communication, etc.

comment   Initiating structure involves leader behaviors initiating
               indicating concern with directing subordinates, structure
               clarifying of roles, establishment of well defined
               patterns and channels of communication and ways of
               getting job done, problem solving, criticizing poor
               work, pressuring subordinates to perform better,
               planning, coordinating, etc.

comment   Leader effectiveness is usually measured by the task
               effective-performance of the leader's work unit, but oth-
               erness supplementary criteria include satisfaction with
               the leader and negative follower behavior such as griev-
               ances, absenteeism, turnover.

comment   While it was generally thought that high consideration
               along patterns with high structure would optimize more
               different effectiveness criteria, and that low considera-
               tion with low structure would minimize effectiveness,
               consistent research results have not demonstrated these
               assumptions.

further study See Fleishman (1973:1–39) Bass (1981:358–92) Yukl
               (1981:105ff)

TWO CATEGORIES OF CONTINGENCY MODELS

introduction   Stogdill's watershed article (1948) forced a paradigm shift from a direct focus on study of leaders (Great Man and Trait Theory) to what leaders do—their behavioral functions. The Ohio State and Michigan studies reduced leadership behavior to two basic generic categories—consideration and initiation of structure. How leaders did these two basic functions became the focus of the next period of leadership research. Leadership style was the topic which described those fundamental ways leaders operated. At the heart of all contingency theory lies the concept of leadership styles. Diagram 1 organizes the categories. Table 1 explains the major items.

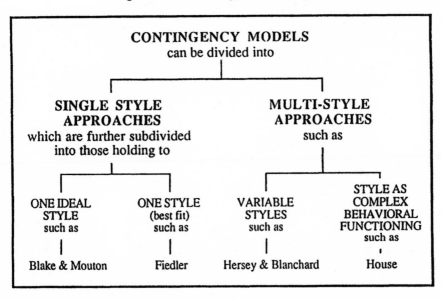

Diagram 1

Theorist	Model	Basic Issue Involved
Blake & Mouton	Managerial Grid	The ideal leadership style is very high in relationship and very high in task. All leaders should strive for this style.
Fiedler	Contingency	A leader's style is related basically to his/her personality and thus can not be changed easily. Hence, one must either adjust the situation to fit that dominant style or change the leader to a situation for which his/her style functions best.
Hersey & Blanchard	Situational	Style is a function not only of situation but also of follower maturity. Different styles are optimally related to different follower maturity levels. A leader can be trained to use a multi-style which fits situation and follower maturity.
House	Path-Goal	Style is contingent on means of influencing toward goals

Table 1

CONTINGENCY MODELS

introduction

Models which see leadership as a dynamic process involving leaders, followers, leader-follower relationships, task, and other situational variables fall into the category called contingency models. The first model which actually went by this name was Fiedler's Contingency Model, but the concept of leadership as a process which is contingent on more than just the leader or his traits or his personality was broader than just Fiedler's Model. Blake and Mouton had devised a model, called the Managerial Grid as early as the mid-fifties which indicated that leadership effectiveness was directly proportional to a best leadership style which integrated a high task focus with a high relationship focus. Fiedler and others held that leaders had styles which were directly a function of personality and hence could not be altered easily. Therefore, for Fiedler effective leadership was contingent on discovering a leader's style and matching it to situational variables in which that style was most effective. Hersey and Blanchard like Blake and Mouton believed that leaders could be trained to utilize different styles but unlike them saw various styles as optimally related to various combinations of follower and situational variables. Other theories like Hollander's Exchange Theory and House's Path Goal were contingency theories in that they did not focus just on leader variables but the heart of their theories relates only obliquely to leadership styles.

definition

Contingency Model is the name given to leadership theories which see leadership effectiveness as contingent upon leadership styles, followers and situational variables.

example   Fiedler's Contingency Model sees effectiveness (where
           effectiveness is primarily performance toward organiza-
           tional goals) as a function of matching one of two
           leadership styles (task-oriented or relations-oriented)
           with two kinds of general situations (favorable and
           unfavorable). Situational favorableness depends on three
           variables: leader-member relations, task structure and
           position power. Task-oriented leaders perform more
           effectively in very favorable and very unfavorable
           situations while relations-oriented leaders perform more
           effectively in situations intermediate in favorableness.

example   Hersey and Blanchard's Life-Cycle Model sees
           leadership effectiveness (where effectiveness is complex
           and primarily a measure of Likert's dependent variables:
           output variables [productivity/ performance],
           intervening variables [the condition of the human
           resources] and short and long range goals) as a function
           of a leader altering various combinations of task and
           relationship behavior to that needed by follower
           maturity.

MANAGERIAL GRID

introduction

In the mid-1960s Blake and Mouton published their book, **The Managerial Grid**. In it was a diagram called "The Managerial Grid," which was a display along an x-y axis. The y axis described "concern for people." It was scaled from 1 (low concern for people) to 9 (high concern for people). The x axis described "concern for production." It was scaled from 1 (low concern for production) to 9 (high concern). While not being exactly the same, these two variables were closely related to "consideration" and "initiating of structure" of the Ohio State model and "task" and "relations" of Fiedler's model. On the diagram were plotted five basic orientations that a leader could have to express how concern for production and concern for people were joined. Mouton and Blake make it clear that though people seem to be predisposed to manage in one way or another, the points on the Grid are not to be thought of as personality types that isolate a given individual's behavior. Identification on the Grid does not slot a person in a rigid and inflexible way. Behavior is flexible and can be changed.

description

The Managerial Grid represents a leadership theory which relates the integration of concern for production with concern for people into five basic clusters each having basic assumptions which will influence leadership style. It advocates high concern for people and high concern for task cluster as the optimum leadership style for effectiveness.

prediction

Managerial effectiveness in organizations is optimum using a leadership style representing the 9,9 plot.

assumptions

1. Three organizational universals include: purpose, people, hierarchy.

2. Theories regarding managerial behavior can be identified according to how these three elements are related.

3. These theories represent sets of assumptions which describe the way a given individual can manage.

4. A given individual's style may be viewed as flowing from a dominant set of assumptions although there are backup assumptions which also influence the style.

5. These assumptions orient the leader as to thinking and behavior in dealing with production/people relationships.

6. Leaders may not be aware of these assumptions.

7. Whenever a person's underlying managerial assumptions change, actual managerial practices also normally shift.

8. Any leader can accept new assumptions and change behavior accordingly.

9. A style, even a dominant one, is not fixed but varies as affected by the following elements: organization, situation, values, personality, chance.

10. Many styles are subject to modification via training.

further study   See Blake & Mouton (1964).

FIEDLER'S CONTINGENCY MODEL

introduction

The leadership theory which has been most dominant throughout leadership history in terms of generating discussion and research has been Fiedler's Contingency Model. It is one of the earliest and certainly best known of the situational theories of leadership. Fiedler, a psychologist by background, did early research which basically tried to predict leader effectiveness using a measure of leader attitudes called the LPC (least preferred co-worker). This was essentially a trait approach to leadership. When he found different results for different kinds of leaders, he developed a contingency theory to explain the discrepancies. The model predicts that high LPC leaders, those with a motivational bias toward close interpersonal relationships, will perform more successfully in situations intermediate in favorableness. Low LPC leaders, with a bias toward achieving tasks, perform more successfully in very favorable and very unfavorable situations.

description

Fiedler's contingency model is a leadership model which predicts effectiveness based on a leader's basic personality orientation toward achievement of task or relationships with followers and/or the leadership situation.

predictions

1. Low (task-oriented) LPC leaders perform better and run more effective groups when there is either very high or very low situational control (that is, the quality of leader-member relationships, the degree of task structure, and the position power of the leader are either altogether highly favorable or altogether highly unfavorable to the leader).

2. High (relations-oriented) LPC leaders are most effective when there is intermediate situational control.

key words **LPC** (least preferred co-worker): is a measure of a leader's basic personality/value orientation.

High LPC: leaders value interpersonal relationship success.

Low LPC: leaders value task success.

Situational control: an analysis of the situation in which the leader and followers work as measured by three items: leader-member relations, task structure, position power.

Leader-member relations: a measure of the leader's influence leverage as related to personal power.

Task structure: a determination of how well defined the goals and operating procedures and evaluation procedures of the group are.

Position Power: a measure of the leader's authority due to position in the organization to use coercive power to bring about compliance.

NINE ASSUMPTIONS UNDERLYING FIEDLER'S
CONTINGENCY MODEL

introduction   While these may not be all the presuppositional assumptions underlying Fiedler's model they are certainly important ones.

Nine Assumptions

1. Leadership effectiveness is essentially a measure of a group's goal performance as directed by a given leader.
2. Leadership effectiveness is dependent on the interaction of leadership style and situational favorableness.
3. A leader's style is a function of his/her personality and is basically fixed and falls dominantly into one of two styles (task oriented or relationship oriented.)
4. A leader's style can be measured.
5. The Least Preferred Co-worker (LPC) instrument measures leadership style.
6. Situational favorableness, the degree to which the situation itself provides the leader with potential power and influence over the group's behavior, is operationally indexed along three component dimensions: leader-member relations, task structure, and position power (Ashour 1973:340).
7. Leader-member relations assumption: A leader who has the loyalty and support of subordinates can depend on them to comply enthusiastically with his/her directions. On the other hand, a leader whose subordinates dislike (or at least disrespect) him/her has no referent power and must be careful that they do not ignore his/her directions or subvert his/her

policies (Yukl 1981:135). Three different measures have been used: leader's rating of the group atmosphere, members' ratings of group atmosphere, and the degree to which the leader is socio-metrically chosen (Ashour 1973:340).

8. Task structure assumptions: A task is highly structured when there is a detailed description of the finished product or service, there are standard operating procedures that guarantee successful completion of the task, and it is easy for the leader to determine how well the work has been performed (Yukl 1981:135). Scales for measuring include goal clarity, decision variability, salvation specificity and goal-path multiplicity (Ashour 1973:340).

9. Position Power Assumption: When a leader has substantial position power, he/she is able to administer rewards and punishments to increase subordinate compliance with his/her directions and policies. Leaders with little or no position power must rely on other sources of influence of behavior (Yukl 1981:135).

Comments   Fiedler has found that leader-member relations are the most important of the three determinants of situational control, followed next by task structure and finally position power (Yukl 1981:135).

Further study   See Ashour (1973), Yukl (1981), Bass (1981:343–357).

HOLLANDER'S EXCHANGE THEORY

introduction

Hollander, in a brief historical reflection, places his own theory of developing parallel to contingency theories.

The lack of generalizability of the trait approach led to two interrelated developments. First was the description of leader behavior, in varying organizational roles. Second, was the situational approach, which emphasized the characteristics of the particular situation and task in which the leaders were mutually involved. The stress was on the demands made for particular leader characteristics.

An extension of the situational approach was the development of contingency models. These models attempted to specify what leader attributes are appropriate, given certain contingencies in the situation. They emphasized factors calling forth different leader qualities to achieve effectiveness.

A parallel development in time was the transactional approach, which considered the quality of the relationship between the leader and followers. The perceptions by followers of the leader's status and legitimacy are significant to this concept. (Hollander 1978:45)

Hollander's theory is basically a transactional one which fuses the situational approach to leadership and the social exchange view of interpersonal relationships.

description

Hollander's Transactional Leadership Theory approaches the study of leadership as a social process of influence involving an ongoing transaction between a leader and followers and has its locus in the overlap among three basal elements (leaders, situation, and followers).

focus   Hollander focuses on the relationship between leader and followers. Legitimacy, authority, status, and bases of influence are key concepts in Hollander's view of leadership.

essential   Some essential ideas underlying Hollander's theory are:

1. Leadership is primarily a process, not a person.
2. Leadership structure provides a framework for the process.
3. The process of leadership involves a social exchange between the leader and followers in a given situation.
4. Leaders provide certain benefits to followers.
5. Followers provide certain support essentials to the leader.
6. Followers' perceptions of the leader's actions and motives are central to a transactional approach.
7. Leadership is a mutual activity in which there usually are both influence and counter-influence.
8. Ability to exert influence is the major operational quality of authority and depends upon transactional processes.

further study   See Hollander (1978), Le Peau (1983).

HERSEY AND BLANCHARD'S SITUATIONAL MODEL
syn: Life Cycle Model

introduction

The basic assumption of Hersey and Blanchard in their situational model is this: The more that managers adapt their style of leader behavior to meet the particular situation and the needs of their followers, the more effective they will tend to be in reaching personal and organizational goals. Hersey and Blanchard define style as "... the behavior pattern that a person exhibits when attempting to influence the activities of others as perceived by those others" (Hersey & Blanchard 1982:95–96). A second quote gives their views on a leader's ability to have different styles and no one best style—issues on which they differ with Fiedler and Mouton/Blake. "In summary, empirical studies tend to show that there is no normative (best) style of leadership. Effective leaders adapt their leader behavior to meet the needs of their followers and the particular environment. If their followers are different, they must be treated differently. Therefore, effectiveness depends on the leader, the follower(s), and other situational variables; $E = f (l,f,s)$. Therefore, anyone who is interested in his or her own success as a leader must give serious thought to these behavioral and environmental considerations" (1982:??).

description

The Hersey-Blanchard Situational Model is a multi-style leadership model which advocates that as leaders vary styles and appropriate power bases according to follower maturity, effectiveness increases.

comment

The Hersey-Blanchard model is depicted as a two dimensional model with the x axis describing task behavior moving from low task to high task toward the right. The y axis describes relational behavior and moves from low at the bottom to high at the top. Four quadrants are thus depicted. The far right lower quadrant represents high task and low behavior and is called the telling leadership style. The far right upper quadrant is high task and high relational and is called the selling leadership style. The far left upper quadrant is high relational and low task and is called the participating leadership style. The far left lower quadrant is low relational and low task and is called the delegating leadership style. Across the x axis at the bottom moving from left to right is a description of follower readiness. To the far left there is high follower readiness; the middle describes moderate readiness; the far right describes low follower readiness. Readiness has to do with ability and motivation. Thus the telling style is for followers with low readiness. The selling and participating for those of moderate readiness and the delegating for those of high readiness.

comment

Situational leadership is based on an interplay among (1) the amount of guidance and direction (task-behavior) a leader gives; (2) the amount of socio-emotional support (relationship behavior) a leader provides; and (3) the readiness (maturity) level that followers exhibit in performing a specific task, function or objective.

further study   See Hersey (1984); Hersey & Blanchard (1982).

HOUSE'S PATH-GOAL LEADERSHIP MODEL

introduction   Bass (1981:444) traces path-goal theory back to research done by Georgopoulos, Mahoney, and Jones in 1957. The theory was popularized by M. G. Evans and Robert J. House. House's (1971) paper, "A Path-Goal Theory of Leader Effectiveness," formalized the model to include situational variables and gave it a wide hearing. The Path-Goal Model is founded on motivational theory (expectancy theory).

description   *The Path Goal Leadership Model* is a situational leadership theory which asserts that leadership behavior (a causal variable) acts to influence subordinate expectancies and valences (intervening variables) to bring about subordinate effort and satisfaction (end-result variables) and is moderated by characteristics of task and subordinates (situational moderator variables).

comment   Yukl (1981:147) diagrams the model as follows:

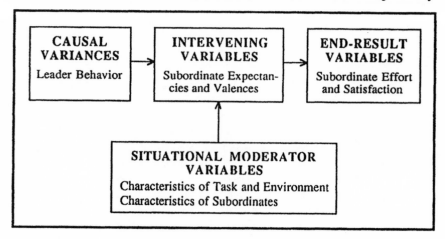

comment   Four kinds of behaviors are described (Yukl 1981:146):

1. Supportive Leadership: behavior that includes giving consideration to the needs of subordinates, displaying concern for their well-being, and creating a friendly climate in the work unit.

2. Directive Leadership: letting subordinates know what they are expected to do, giving specific guidance, asking subordinates to follow rules and procedures, scheduling and coordinating the work.

3. Participative Leadership: consulting with subordinates and taking their opinions and suggestions into account when making decisions.

4. Achievement-Oriented Leadership: setting challenging goals, seeking performance improvements, emphasizing excellence in performance, and showing confidence that subordinates will attain high standards.

further study   See Yukl (1981:144–153) House (1971).

VROOM-YETTON NORMATIVE DECISION MAKING
LEADERSHIP MODEL

introduction

Two models are given in this map. One is the overall framework on which Vroom-Yetton analyze leadership research. The second is their model applied to decision-making. Their assumptions are given in the following quote:

> We set out to examine leader behavior both normatively and descriptively. The two questions, "How should leaders behave if they are to be effective?" and "How do they behave?" have been in the background of all of the work presented in the previous nine chapters. Since one cannot effectively examine all aspects of leader behavior simultaneously, we chose one aspect that, on the basis of previous work, was likely to be of major importance. We selected the leader's role in the decision-making process ... (Vroom & Yetton 1973:197).

Yukl (1981:224) says, "The Vroom and Yetton model appears to be a promising development in leadership theory." He does not speak this highly of any other leadership model.

description

The Vroom-Yetton leadership research framework model is a model which seeks to evaluate leadership study under five major elements: personal attributes, leader behavior, organizational effectiveness and two types of situational variables.

description

The Vroom-Yetton normative leadership decision making model is a model which uses the leadership research framework model above and limits leader behavior to decision processes.

comment   Vroom & Yetton describe their model schematically as follows.

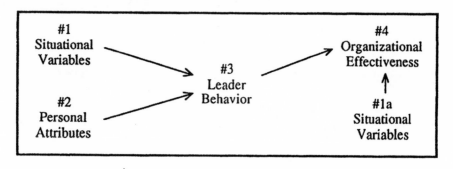

comment   The key variable (or set of variables) in the figure is labeled #3, leader behavior—the actions or behaviors exhibited by the leader in the course of carrying out his leadership role. The decision process used by the leader is one (and only one) of the variables that might be used in the analysis of such behavior. With respect to #1 and #2, Leadership Behavior is the dependent variable and is studied using descriptive methodology. With respect to #4, Leader Behavior and #1a Situational Variables are independent variables and #4 Organizational Effectiveness is the dependent variable. The inter-relation of these variables is studied using normative methodology.

further study See Vroom & Yetton (1973) Yukl (19871) Hill & Schmidt (1977).

YUKL'S MULTIPLE LINKAGE MODEL OF LEADER EFFECTIVENESS

introduction

Yukl, in order to provide a more comprehensive theory of leadership which took into account situational moderator variables and intervening variables at the same time, posited his Multiple Linkage Model in 1971. It has since been modified to include a larger number of intervening variables and to include a wider range of more specific leadership behaviors. In addition to a leader's short-term influence on the intervening variables the model also recognizes the leader's longer term capacity to modify situational variables as a means of improving group performance (Yukl 1981:153).

description

Yukl's Multi-linkage Model is a situational leadership model which sees leadership behavior (a causal variable) acting immediately to influence intervening variables (six given) and acting long term to change situational variables (three different categories distinguished) in order to bring about subordinate performance.

comment

See Yukl (1981:161) for a schematic of the model.

explanation:

The Yukl model is a six component model: 1. Leader behavior, 2. situational constraints on leader behavior, 3. intervening variable, 4. situational variables directly affecting the intervening variables, 5. situational variables that determine the priority of intervening variable and 6. subordinate performance. It is a complex diagram with leader behavior directly affecting components 2, 3, 4, 5 and in turn being affected by 2. Components 4 directly affects 3. Component 5 affects 6. This is a very complex model with high level abstraction.

comment   Major propositions underlying the model:

1. A leader's short-term effectiveness depends on the extent to which he/she acts skillfully to correct any deficiencies in the intervening variables for his/her work unit.

2. The situation determines which intervening variables are most important, which ones are in need of improvement, and what potential corrective actions are available to the leader.

3. Over a longer time period, leaders can act to change some of the situational variables and create a more favorable situation.

further study   See Yukl (1981).

Appendix C.

List of Prominent Leadership Influentials

LIST OF PROMINENT LEADERSHIP INFLUENTIALS

The asterisk indicates a career profile has been completed.

Adams*, Richard
Adelman*, Frederick J.
Adizes*, Ichak
Adorno*, Theodor W.
Allen*, Louis A.
Argyris*, Chris
Armerding*, Hudson Taylor
Barber*, Cyril John
Barnard*, C. I.
Bass*, Bernard M.
Beloin*, Robert L.
Bennis*, Warren G.
Blake*, Robert R.
Blanchard*, K. H.
Blankenship, L. V.
Blau*, Peter M.
Bogardus*, Emory S.
Borman*, Ernest and Nancy
Bowers, D. G.
Burger*, Peter
Burns*, James MacGregor
Butt*, Howard Edward, Jr.
Campbell*, Dennis Marion
Carlyle*, Thomas
Cartwright*, Desmond Spencer
Cartwright*, Dorin

Chemers*, Martin M.
Culbert*, Samuel Alan
Dominian*, Jack (Jacob)
Drucker*, Peter Ferdinand
England*, George William
Engstrom*, Theodore Wilhelm
Etzioni*, Amitai Werner
Farrow, D. L.
Fiedler*, Fred Edward
Fleishman*, Edwin Alan
Flint, A. W.
Gangel*, Kenneth O.
Ghiselli, E. E.
Gibb*, C. A. (Cecil)
Glaser*, B. G.
Graen, G.
Greene, C. N.
Gruenfeld, L. W.
Guest, R. H.
Guetzkow, H.
Gustafson*, James
Halpin, A. W.
Hamblin, R. L.
Hare, A. P.
Heller, F. A.
Hemphill*, J. K.
Henderson*, Ian

Hitt*, Russell T.
Hocking*, David L.
Hodges*, Melvin
Hollander*, Edwin P.
Horne*, H. H.
House*, Robert J.
Hull*, Raymond
Hunt*, James G.
Jennings, H. H.
Jones*, Ezra Earl
Kahn, R. L.
Katz, D.
Kerr, S.
Lanzetta, J. T.
Larson, L. L.
Lawler, E. E.
Likert*, Renis
Lippitt, R.
Maier, N. R. F.
Mann, F. C.
Maslow*, Abraham
McCall, M. W. Jr.
McClelland, D. C.
McConkey, Dale D.
McDonough*, Reginald M.
McGregor*, Douglas
McGregor*, Douglas
McMurry*, Robert N.
Merton, R. K.
Miller, J. A.
Miner, J. B.
Mintzberg*, Henry
Mitchell, T. R.
Mouton, J. S.
Nadler*, Leonard
Nadler*, Zeace
Newcomb, T. M.

Odiorne*, George Stanley
Oldham, G. R.
Osborn, R. N.
Paige*, Glenn D.
Patchen, M.
Pelz, D. C.
Penner, D. D.
Pepinsky, P. N.
Peter*, Laurence J.
Petty, M. M.
Pfiffner, J. M.
Porter, L. W.
Powers*, Bruce P.
Pryer, M. W.
Raven, B. H.
Rice, R. W.
Roby, T. B.
Rohde, K. J.
Russell*, Bertrand
Ryterband, E. C.
Sample, J. A.
Sanders*, J. Oswald
Schaller*, Lyle
Schein, E. H.
Schriesheim, C. A.
Schriesheim, J. F.
Scott, E. L.
Seashore, S. E.
Seeman, M.
Shartle*, C. L.
Shaw, M. E.
Sims, H. P.
Slocum, J. W.
Smith, M.
Solem, A. R.
Solomon, R. J.
Steiner, I. D.
Stinson, J. E.

Stogdill*, Ralph M.
Stouffer, S. A.
Strauss*, A. L.
Strodtbeck, F. L.
Szilagyi, A. D.
Tannebaum, A. S.
Tannebaum, R.
Thelen, H. A.
Thibaut, J. W.
Torrance, E. P.
Triandis, H. C.
Tryon, C. M.
Valenzi, E. R.
Vroom*, Victor H.
Weschler, I. R.
Westie, C. W.
Whyte, W. F.
Wilson, T. R.
Wood, M. M.
Wurster, C. R.
Yetton , P. W.
Yukl*, Gary A.
Zaleznik, A.
Zander, A.
Zeleny, L. D.

Printed in the United States
75968LV00002B/4

9 781932 814187